# Be Different

*Cycle A Sermons for Advent, Christmas, and Epiphany
Based on the Gospel Texts*

## John B. Jamison

CSS Publishing Company, Inc.

Lima, Ohio

BE DIFFERENT

*Cycle A Sermons for Advent, Christmas, and Epiphany Based on the Gospel Texts*

FIRST EDITION

Copyright © 2019

by CSS Publishing Co., Inc.

**Library of Congress Cataloging-in-Publication Data**

Names: Jamison, John B., 1952- author. Title: Be different : Cycle A sermons for Advent, Christmas, and Epiphany based on the Gospel texts / John B. Jamison. Description: First edition. | Lima, Ohio : CSS Publishing Company, Inc., [2019] Identifiers: LCCN 2019002491 | ISBN 9780788029875 (pbk. : alk. paper) | ISBN 0788029878 (pbk.) | ISBN 9780788029882 (ebk.) | ISBN 0788029886 (ebk.) Subjects: LCSH: Bible. Matthew--Sermons. | Common lectionary (1992). Year A. | Advent sermons. | Christmas sermons. | Epiphany season--Sermons. | Church year sermons. | Sermons, American--21st century. Classification: LCC BS2575.54 .J36 2019 | DDC 252/.61--dc23

For more information about CSS Publishing Company resources, visit our website at www.csspub .com, email us at csr@csspub.com, or call (800) 241-4056.

e-book:
ISBN-13: 978-0-7880-2988-2
ISBN-10: 0-7880-2988-6

ISBN-13: 978-0-7880-2987-5

ISBN-10: 0-7880-2987-8

PRINTED IN USA

To all of those who helped teach me the story.

# Contents

# INTRODUCTION

I have two goals for writing this book; one for you and one for me. For you, my goal is to offer a preachable collection of story ideas that leave room for you to adapt and make them fit your style and your listener's needs. For me, my goal is to continue to try and better understand just what my faith is calling me to do and be. I know my faith calls me to be different, but how? Different from what?

The sermons in this book are some of my attempts to understand that call to difference. My hope is that these story-sermons might give you something to work with, to adapt and present as you continue to tell the most important story.

Preach on!

Advent 1

Matthew 24:36-44

# Christmas Is Out Of Control

After hearing the scripture reading, the thought going through your head may be, "What the heck does that have to do with Christmas? Isn't this the first Sunday of Advent? Why are you talking about Noah? And didn't Jesus say those things during holy week, like on Palm Sunday? Where is the Christmas story?"

Let me try to explain. There is a thing called the lectionary; some of you are probably familiar with it. The lectionary is a list of scriptures for each Sunday of the year, and other special days as well. It's not a new idea. According to the Jewish Talmud, they used a set list of readings for festivals and services all the way back in Moses' day. Today's scripture reading from Matthew is one of the passages on the lectionary list for the first Sunday of Advent this year. That's why we're reading it today.

Now, you may be wondering why we use something like the lectionary? Can't we pick out our own scriptures? Do we really need somebody to tell us what to preach about? Do we have to use this lectionary thing, or what? No, not everyone uses the lectionary. But there are a couple of benefits that come from preaching from the lectionary.

First, the people who create the lectionary try to select passages that fit logical patterns. The passages fit together with a theme, showing how passages from the Old Testament, the gospels, and the epistles can all work together.

Second, the lists include scriptures from all parts of the Bible, so over the year, we are hearing from the entire story, rather than just a few favorite pieces we might like to talk about. And, honestly, this can sometimes make preaching more difficult. Sometimes, the passage on the list is one that we might not choose to preach about if it was left up to us.

For some preachers, this passage from Matthew is one of those difficult ones. Preachers and churches that talk a lot about the end of time love this passage and are happy to see it on today's list. Those who don't talk much about the end, well, this can be a tough day.

But back to question: Why did the lectionary people select this passage to start off the Advent season? Let me see if I can help make some sense out of it.

To do that, let me start with a story.

The story began a day or two after Palm Sunday, with Jesus back in the temple in Jerusalem. All of his disciples were standing around him to hear what he had to say. When they first got there on Sunday, he ended up throwing things around, calling people names, and creating quite a stir, so the disciples were curious what this day would bring. I want you to keep one eye on the disciple called Simon. Not Simon Peter the fisherman, but the other Simon, the one called Simon Zelotes. He was the one standing out at the edge of the group, looking around.

He seemed to be paying more attention to what was going on around the temple instead of focusing on what Jesus was saying. And, you might notice that Simon had one hand tucked inside his robe.

Simon Zelotes was not called that because he was from a town called Zelotes like Mary Magdalene was from Magdala. He was given that name because he belonged to a group called the Zealots. The Zealots were a political group that had the one goal of driving the Romans out of the country and retaking control of their kingdom. The Zealots were militant and wanted to incite a full rebellion and get rid of the Romans by force if necessary. Because of that, every zealot carried a small sword with them at all times, hoping to get an opportunity to stick it in a Roman centurion. That's what Simon was holding onto under his robe; his sword. He was looking around the temple at the centurion guards. According to historians, during religious festivals like Passover, there was a Roman centurion stationed at every column around the temple. The entire temple courtyard was lined with columns, so Simon was looking at a lot of bright red centurions. And after what Jesus had done the day before, most of those centurions were looking right back at Simon and his group. Along with the centurions, the courtyard was filled with groups of Pharisees, Sadducees, priests, and scribes; Jews in positions of power who kept that power because they went along with the Romans. The Zealots hated them almost as much as the Romans themselves. Simon looked nervous but excited. He had waited for this day for a very long time.

According to Matthew, Jesus began talking to his disciples, and anyone else nearby, telling them a couple of parables. He didn't turn over tables that day, but his stories had a way of getting the point across, and most of them pointed directly at those Pharisees, Sadducees, priests, and scribes. It didn't take long before they had heard enough. A group of Pharisees walked over to where Jesus was standing and smiled. They said:

"Teacher, we know that you are true, and teach the way of God truthfully, and do not regard the position of men."

Have you ever had that happen? Someone walks up and is all smiley-faced and sweet-talking, but you know full-well that they're just setting you up? Yeah. Jesus just looked at them as they continued:

"Tell us what you think. Is it lawful to pay taxes to Caesar, or not?"

They smiled. They had him now. If he said it was lawful to pay the taxes, he was showing support for Rome. That would anger the zealots. But if he said it was not lawful to pay the taxes, he was speaking open rebellion against Rome, and that would bring the Centurions. That's what Pharisees do. Their job is to keep track of all of the Jewish laws, all the way back to the time of Moses. And there was a pile of laws after several hundred years. Making it even more difficult was the fact that any rabbi could give his own interpretation to the laws, and each of those interpretations became kind of a law itself. As you read the old books you find a lot of: "Rabbi Gamaliel says… but Rabbi Schmalich says… and Rabbi Gelbin says…" all depending on how each rabbi interpreted the original law.

So no matter what you said or did, if a Pharisee wanted to, he could easily find some reason to catch you breaking a law. That's how they kept people under control. They played a very good game of "Gotcha!" That's what they were doing with Jesus. No matter what he answered: "Gotcha!"

In my mind, Jesus smiled. He knew the game of "Gotcha!" He looked at the group of very proud and smiling Pharisee-snakes, and asked: "Who's picture is on the money?"

The Pharisees paused a minute, a bit confused at his response, and finally said, "Caesar's picture."

Jesus shrugged and said, "Then, give to Caesar what belongs to Caesar, and give to God what belongs to God."

The Pharisees glanced at each other, then at Jesus, then back at each other, then over at the group of Sadducees who had been watching the whole thing, then just kind of walked away. Their trap did not work.

The Sadducees smiled a snarky little smile as the Pharisees walked past. The two groups disagreed on lots of things, but the biggest difference between them was that while the Pharisees all came from middle-class Jewish families, the Sadducees all came from the upper crust, from the rich and powerful privileged families. The Sadducees believed that God gave people what they deserved, so the rich were rich because God thought they were better than the people who were poor. Plus, the Sadducees did not believe in the idea of a resurrection Jesus had talked about. As the Sadducees walked over to Jesus they had two goals: one was to catch Jesus, and the other was to embarrass the Pharisees. The Sadducees were also good with laws, especially theological laws, so they came up with a really good "Gotcha!"

They said, "Suppose a man dies with no children, and his brother marries the widow to raise children for his brother's sake."

That was one of the old laws created to make sure a family lineage continued even if a man died before he had children. Although it sounds really strange to us now, so far they were just stating a fact.

The Sadducee continued: "But what if there are seven brothers, and they all die? So, the widow actually ends up marrying all seven of them. In this resurrection you talk about…who is married to who?"

Again, in my imagination, Jesus smiled as they waited. They were ready for any answer he might give.

Except for the one he gave them. "You people don't understand the resurrection at all, do you?"

While the Sadducees mumbled among themselves trying to come up with a suitable retort, the Pharisees came back for another shot, pushing the Sadducees out of the way.

They said, "Teacher, what is the greatest commandment?"

Usually, when you called someone "teacher" it was a sign of respect. This time it was pure sarcasm.

Jesus smiled again. This was a good one. There were ten commandments and different groups believed that different commandments were the most important. No matter which one he chose, he was going to make someone mad.

He paused briefly and said, "You shall love the Lord your God with all your heart, and with all your soul, and with all your mind."

One of the Pharisees started to respond, but Jesus kept going.

"And a second is like it, 'You shall love your neighbor as yourself.' On these two commandments depend all the law and the prophets."

The Pharisees smiled as one of them started to point out that neither of those two things was actually one of the Ten Commandments, but that's when things changed.

I think the smile left Jesus' face as he took a step toward and looked at both the Pharisees and Sadducees. Matthew doesn't include it, but in my imagination, Jesus begins with "And now I've got one for you…"

He said, "What do you think of the Christ? Whose son is he?"

Both Pharisees and Sadducees smiled at this youngster challenging the experts.

"The son of David."

This was Law 101. Any entry level Pharisee or Sadducee could answer it. Can you see the smirks on their faces?

"How is it, then," Jesus said, "David called him 'Lord' instead of 'son'?"

They all recognized the phrase from Psalm 110. The Pharisees glanced at the Sadducees. The Sadducees glanced at the Pharisees. They all began to debate and argue.

Matthew says, "No one was able to answer him a word, nor from that day did anyone dare to ask him any more questions."

But Jesus was just getting started. He spent the next few minutes talking to each of the groups standing there; the Pharisees, the Sadducees, the priests, and the scribes.

"Woe to you..." he said, describing them as hypocrites who use their position for wealth and power, instead of for mercy and faith. He said they were like somebody who polishes the outside of a cup but leaves the inside all moldy and messy. He said they were like someone who strained the gnat out of wine, but swallowed a camel. He said they looked beautiful on the outside, but on the inside, they were like a pile of dead man's bones. He said they were like "blind guides," and when they teach someone to follow them, what they are actually doing is creating another "child of hell."

Jesus then paused, looked around the entire temple area, said something about the true desolation that was there, and then walked away. As he left the courtyard, apparently one of the disciples made a comment about how grand the temple building was. Jesus turned to him and said: "Truly I say to you, there will not be one stone upon another that will not be thrown down."

He then walked down the path, across the Kidron stream, and up the Mount of Olives to the place they were staying. As they walked, Jesus tried to explain more about what was going to happen.

Can you see Simon's face now? In my mind, he keeps looking behind them to see if anyone was following them. His hand was on his sword. He wanted to be ready.

That evening Jesus tried to explain to them what was going to happen. At one point, someone asked Jesus when it would be; when was the new kingdom finally going to come?

Matthew tells us a lot of what Jesus said, but in short, he said, "Dad is the only one who knows, and he's not talking. What is important is that you are ready for whenever it does happen."

And that's when I imagine Simon stood up, pulled his little sword from his robe, and said proudly: "Don't' worry Lord, we are ready! We will drive the Romans out, and those that won't be driven away will meet the edge of our swords!"

Everyone cheered — except Jesus. Leave Simon for a moment and look at Jesus' face. The expression that says, "Again? They still don't understand. How many times have I tried to teach them?"

How many times had Jesus explained that what he was offering was a not just another political kingdom, but was an end of the corruption of the temple, an end of all of the unjust laws; a different kind of kingdom?

Still, after all this time, they did not understand.

But honestly, we can't blame them...or fault them...

I think we can all relate to what it felt like living under the pressures; the constant threat of being attacked or criticized for breaking some rule that we did not create; the corrupt leaders who spoke words of justice while performing acts of injustice.

I think some of us have talked about the day the pendulum will swing, and we will retake control of our kingdom. The day those now with power will see what it feels like to be powerless and will experience our version of justice. That day when we will drive out our modern Pharisees, Sadducees, scribes, and priests, all of those controlling our lives, and it will be our time to repay them.

No, I don't think we can blame them…or fault them.

Many of us have dreamed of the day we will take our steps to make the world great again. We will, once again, be in control.

We still do not understand. It is not about control. It is not about controlling others by playing "gotcha!" with laws to keep others in their place, or away from our place. It is not about retaking control or welcoming a nice, new kingdom that gives us that control and opportunity to repay others.

It is something bigger.

And it is not important for us to worry about when change will take place.

Our task is to simply be ready. And that simply means to love God, and love your neighbor as you love yourself… no more, no less. That is what it means to be ready. That is all we can do. That is all that we control.

But, going all the way back to where we started, what does this have to do with Christmas?

Again, to me, it all comes down to control.

We have Christmas under control. No swords nowadays…but schedules, plans, menus, gifts…we raise our lists and announce: "We're ready Lord, come on in! We started shopping, stocking store shelves back in September and we have done everything we could do to make sure we can have a Christmas that goes smoothly, and fits right in with our expectations, and won't disrupt things too awfully much. We have it under control."

Over the next few weeks, we are going to remind ourselves that the real message of Christmas is a message of surprise! It's like magic... something unexpected... something new...something out of our control.

So, plan your travels... plan your meals... plan your gifts... all the rest of it to prepare for another merry, and controlled, Christmas.

But, just be ready....

Amen.

# Have A Very Messy Christmas!

I'll tell you, this had to be something to see. The Jordan River is not a big river like many that we might think of. At its widest, you could still easily thrown a stone across it, and in many other places, you could just step from one side to the other. The wide and deeper spots usually became places where people would gather to fill their water jugs, wash clothes, bathe the children... or just escape from the heat and dryness of the land around the river. Most of the land was a wilderness; narrow paths leading through rocky hills and steep canyons, scattered scrub brush, and the occasional old tree whose roots had found some kind of moisture. There were snakes and scorpions and robbers, but the greatest threat was the land itself. In the wilderness, your body lost a quart of water an hour simply by breathing. So the river, even the small one, was a place that people were drawn to. So, if you had something you wanted to tell people about, the river was a good place to go.

And today, standing out in the middle of the river, with the muddy water swirling around his knees, is a man. Matthew told us the familiar story of John; John the Baptist. He was standing out there wearing what looked like a burlap bag, with a leather belt wrapped around his waist. He was wet, his hair hanging down, and overall he looked, well, he looked a mess. He spent most of his time in the wilderness, eating the things found there like wild honey, locusts, so he was thin, wet, and he was waving his arms and screaming at people lining up along both sides of the river banks.

And the people were there, lots of them. Matthew said they came from Jerusalem, which at its closest was more than twenty miles through some really nasty territory. It's the land where the man was attacked, beaten, and left for dead until that good samaritan came along. But they came from Jerusalem, from all of Judea, Matthew said from the whole region of the Jordan…which stretched almost one hundred forty miles from the Sea of Galilee in the north to the Dead Sea in the south. They came to confess their sins and be baptized in that muddy, Jordan River, by the man in the burlap bag.

John had been doing this for a while, and he certainly had a following. We know he must have been important because Matthew told us the Pharisees and Sadducees had even come down from Jerusalem to hear him. These were the key religious leaders from the temple, and if they walked all the way down there John must have been saying and doing something that had gotten their attention. Through the years there were perhaps hundreds of men running around preaching and calling themselves prophets, and most of them were shrugged off by the temple. But John — there was something about John that had gotten their attention, something that brought them all the way to the river.

We know the story. John saw the proud Pharisees and Sadducees standing there in their robes and hats, looking so smug and pious. That was usually enough. Those men in their robes held a tremendous amount of power. They interpreted and enforced the laws, the old laws from Moses and the scrolls filled with new laws, so many that if you angered a Pharisee or Sadducee they had no trouble at all finding a law you had violated and making you pay severely for it. Everyone feared the men in the robes. None of the other people standing on the riverbank that day were happy to see them there.

We don't know if any of them actually got into the water to be baptized, but John lit into them anyway. "You bunch of snakes!" he said. In my imagination there was a scattering of applause from the crowd on both sides of the river, common folks just happy to hear someone finally call a snake a snake. John went on to really tell them off, telling them that their fancy robes and their high-falootin' positions weren't worth anything at all to God, even if they could trace their family tree all the way back to Moses himself. I can hear them yelling back with their theological rebuttals, but John had no time or interest in theology. "The ax is already at the root of the trees," he said. "And branches like you that don't produce anything worthwhile are going to be thrown in the wood chipper and used for mulch!" Forgive me if I kind of updated some of what he said there.

If John was around today he would have his own reality television show:

"This week on The Baptizer: John is confronted by an angry Pharisee who traveled all the way from Jerusalem. But this time, the Pharisee brings his buddies. Will John finally back down? Or is the Pharisee and his friends about to get an education in riverside theology? Find out this Thursday night on The Baptizer!"

John the Baptist is a familiar story. Today, when we talk about John we usually talk about what happened that day when Jesus came to the river and ended up being baptized by John. We often see that as the beginning of Jesus ministry, the day everything changed. We celebrate the fact that John truly prepared the way for Jesus to begin his ministry, and set the stage for what Jesus was about to do.

That's the familiar story. But there is actually more to it than that.

The familiar story seems to suggest that when Jesus came out of the river after being baptized by John, John stepped back and let Jesus take over the work he had been doing. As the "preparer," now that Jesus was there, John's work was completed. He could retire, or at least take an advisory position on Jesus team to help bring about all the things John had been preaching about for so many years. But that's not what happened.

There is more to the story. It isn't that clean and neat.

If we read what the other gospel writers say about John, we find things that Matthew doesn't tell us about. For example, Matthew wasn't interested in where John was from, or really interested in just who John was. The other writers tell us more about John, and that sometimes makes our familiar story a little messy.

John was more than just a guy who showed up and baptized Jesus at the river that day. John's birth had a miracle to it as well. Luke told us that John's parents, Elizabeth and Zechariah, were too old to have children. Zechariah was a priest at the temple, and one day while he was inside changing the candles, Luke said an angel appeared and told him Elizabeth was going to have a baby. Even though Zechariah was a priest, he had a hard time believing the news and told the angel that. Here is a word of advice... never argue with an angel. The angel looked at Zechariah and said something like, "Well, okay then. You want proof? From now until the baby is born you are not going to be able to speak. Not a word. How's that for proof?" Zechariah tried to apologize but nothing came out. Nine months later, John arrived, along with Zechariah's voice. Luke let us know that John was more than just another preacher... there was something more.

Luke also told us that Elizabeth and Mary were related. We're not exactly sure how. Some believe that Jesus and John were cousins, though there is nothing that says that. Some people then ask, if they were cousins, then why didn't John recognized him when he came to the river to be baptized. We'll save that debate for another day. Let's just say Luke has made our familiar story a bit messier.

Another tradition from the historians is that, because of their ages, John became an orphan. Some believe he was then adopted by a group known as the Essenes. The Essenes were a religious community that disagreed with the temple and spent their time writing and praying about the time when the real Messiah would arrive and the temple would be overthrown. Some believe that's where John learned to be the preacher he became. The Essenes also used baptism as the sign of being pure and clean, which some say also explained John's actions. But the Essenes were very private, not the kind of people who would draw crowds to the river. So, did John start there and then leave for some reason? Or, are the historians just mistaken? Again… messy.

The other thing we learned about John from the other gospel writers and historians is that the transition from John to Jesus was not quite as smooth and clean-cut as we imagined. John did not stop his work when Jesus started his. In fact, Jesus told us that John was a prophet and was actually Elijah, the one who would announce the coming of the Messiah. But in the gospel of John, John stated that he was not a prophet and was not Elijah. While Jesus began his ministry, John continued his. The gospels even described a time when John's disciples and Jesus' disciples got into an argument about why John's disciples fasted and Jesus' disciples did not. If we look at all of the material about John, it seems that not only did John continue his ministry, but there may have been times that John and Jesus were at odds, running competing ministries.

One day Jesus was asked about John and he said that John was a great man, but that "the least in the kingdom was greater than him." This could be one of Jesus' philosophical statements that needed to be thought about to understand, or, could it be a bit of frustration that no matter how great John may be, when it comes to the real kingdom, he's not *that* great? Again, we'll leave this to the theologians to debate. But at this point, it just makes our familiar story of John the Baptist messier.

John's followers continued even after his death. His bones were gathered, became relics, and are still found in several different shrines around the world. While Jesus is recognized as the foundation of the Christian faith, John is still a central figure in the religious community called the Mandaens. According to another current tradition, in 1829 John returned to meet with a group in Pennsylvania.

While Matthew clearly presented John as the preparer, and even had John saying that the one coming after him was more powerful, when we listen to what the others say the whole story is a bit messier. What do we do with all this, and maybe more importantly, why am I telling you all of this? Why am I messing up a perfectly nice little story?

I actually have two reasons.

First, is to recognize how difficult it sometimes is to be number two. I don't know if John actually did end up competing with Jesus or at least had a hard time giving up his high-profile role, but I can certainly understand it if he did. I understand how difficult it can sometimes be in relationships, like marriage. What happens when one or both people forget that their role is to support and care for the other and not to simply demand to be respected as the top dog. I understand how easy it can be for parents to forget that their role as mother or father is in first place for a time, and it will be a while before their world becomes their own again.

Being number two is difficult. If John struggled with it I fully understand. And, if John did struggle with it, then maybe I'm not so bad when I do the same thing. There's hope.

And what is the second thing I take from this - the second reason I've messed up the story today? It's because faith is messy. We sometimes get the idea that if we have enough faith, or the correct faith, then everything gets a little easier, smoother, and more comfortable. I have heard preachers say that. I have heard people say that if you have faith, problems will go away, money will come in, and life will be easier. If I have faith, the messes will go away.

Jesus never said that.

Faith is messy. Faith doesn't provide easy answers. Faith doesn't clean everything up. What faith does, for me, is remind me that no matter how messy things get, no matter how confused, how difficult things become, I am doing what I can do, I am doing the best I can do. We can leave the debating about the messes to the theologians, and just focus on living our lives. We just do our best.

You see, it really doesn't matter if John had trouble giving up his position. It doesn't really matter if John and Jesus had problems or not. The reality is that God was still able to use them to get done what needed to get done. God doesn't seem to be all that concerned about messes.

I think that's a good point to end on as we begin this second week of Advent. Christmas is coming. Some of us have spent a lot of time and energy to make sure this Christmas goes smoothly. Haven't we? Meals, visitors, programs, travels, relatives... *relatives*... we are spending a lot of time and energy to make sure things don't get messy this year. We're not going to let anyone or anything ruin Christmas this year! We will spend so much time and energy that we're not going to relax again until it's all over, presents are unwrapped and everyone has gone back home.

Just keep in mind, messes are a part of this journey. Messes are a part of our faith. Messes don't have to ruin anything. No matter the mess, it's Christmas. Relax a bit. Do your best, but expect a mess or two. And when they happen, smile. Love God. Love those around you.

Leave all the rest to God.

Amen.

Matthew 11:2-11

# John And Frank

Have you ever had doubts about what you believe? I mean really had doubts? You were so certain of everything, but over time questions started arising. Or maybe something happened that shook you really hard, and you began to wonder if all that you believed in was real? Can you relate to that at all?

That's where we find John in today's scripture. He had spent so many years being the powerful preacher, the one proclaiming his faith that everything was about to change for the better. His beliefs had given him the strength to stand up against the most powerful groups of the day. He spoke truth, even when truth was a dangerous thing to speak. People traveled from all over the country to come and hear what he had to say. They listened to him, and they gained strength in their own faith because of him. Even after Jesus was baptized and began his ministry, people still kept coming to hear John. They saw him as the example of what it meant to believe in God.

But then things changed.

History isn't fully clear about what happened. Some historians say that the point had finally come when the religious and political leaders finally decided that John had to be silenced. They could have just arrested him to shut him up, as they had done with many others. But John had so many followers, more than any of the others, they were afraid of what mischief he still might be able to create from jail. He could still get messages to his followers. Their only option was to kill him. So, this tradition says John was arrested and put in prison where he would be killed and silenced for good.

Other historians give a different version of what happened. This tradition says the decision to arrest John was made, reluctantly, by the Roman Governor, Herod Antipas. Herod knew about John. He had even had a dream that John was raised from the dead. Although John was a problem, Herod was hesitant to do anything like arresting or killing him. Dreams were thought to be significant, and even Roman governors don't like to take too many chances with that kind of thing. While those around him argued that John should die, Herod waited. Even when John made an insulting comment about Herod marrying Herodias, the wife of his brother Philip, certainly grounds for a Roman ruler to act, Herod left John alone. But one night there was a party for Herod, and one of the entertainments was a dance by Herodias' daughter. Herod thought the dance was so wonderful, he called the young girl over and said to thank her he would give her anything her little heart desired. Anything at all. The girl had a brief conversation with her mother, who was still angry about what John had said about her. The daughter returned to Herod and said the only thing she wanted was the head of John the Baptist. Herod had no choice but to honor his word. John was arrested and thrown into a prison cell on a mountain out on the edge of the wilderness, far from where he could cause any more trouble, where he was to be killed.

And that's where we find John today.

It is worth noting that, when we say John was in a prison cell, what we actually mean was that he was sitting at the bottom of a big hole cut some thirty feet into the ground. The only opening was a little door in the ceiling where they threw you in, and where they lowered the rope later to pull you out so they could kill you. Or they just left you there. The hole was never cleaned, there was no light, so just let your imagination run with that for a few minutes. Can you see John sitting there? Can you hear what was going on in his mind?

It reminds me of Frank. Frank was a leader in his church and his community. Frank had spent his life doing whatever he could do to help others. He gave his money to help others. He gave his time to help others. Frank believed it was important for him to treat everyone he met as someone who had real value, regardless of their position in life or mistakes they may have made. Everyone respected Frank and saw him as an example of what it meant to lead a life of faith.

Frank was never sick, nothing worse than a case of the flu or something similar. Everyone said it was because Frank led such a good and faithful life - until he was 75. Frank woke up one morning and felt a pain. He went to the doctor and after running tests, they found that Frank had developed cancer. They began the treatments immediately, and even though it was difficult, Frank remained the picture of a man of faith. But after a while, as the side effects of his treatments increased, Frank began to grow more quiet. He stayed home more, explaining that he was tired and needed to focus his energy on getting better. But it was more than that. Frank's family told their pastor that Frank was not just tired, he was getting more and more angry by the day. He had stopped talking with them. He just sat in his room and stared at his shoes. The pastor came to visit and Frank had had enough. He looked his pastor in the eyes and said, "Why me? What did I do? I thought I was doing the Lord's work. Why me?"

Frank felt like he was sitting in a deep, dark, hole. He hadn't done all of the good things he had done in his life to earn some type of award, but come on, is this how it is supposed to go? Is this what faith gets you? We may shake our heads and say, "That's not how it works. He should have known better," but that is an easy thing to say from out here. When you find yourself in a hole surrounded by darkness, only then can we really understand Frank and John. Is this really how it was supposed to go? Did I miss something? Did I really do the right things? What did I do wrong? There are a lot of questions.

Matthew tells us that John sent some of his disciples to find Jesus and ask, "Are you really the one, or should we expect someone else?" John and Frank wanted to know, are you really the one, or did I misunderstand things and make a mistake with my life? I think many of us have understood that question, maybe even asked it a few times. How do we know we are doing the right thing?

How do we know we are living our lives in a meaningful way? And if we are doing the right thing, then why is life so difficult at times?

John's disciples found Jesus and asked him the question.

'Am I the one?" Jesus said, "Just look around you. Look at the number people standing in line to talk with me, and the lines over there of people wanting me to autograph my latest book. Look at our facilities. Our synagogue services are the largest in the entire area, and that is without counting all of our satellite centers where people can gather to hear me over our broadband multimedia network. Look at our budget; the amount we collected for missions in the last six months alone. We have more members than every other synagogue in the land, combined. You go and tell John that."

Of course, that's not what Jesus said, though I've heard it said many other times by others. When John's disciples asked Jesus if he was really the one, he said:

"Go back and tell John what you hear and see. The blind receive sight, the lame walk, those who have leprosy are cleansed, the deaf hear, the dead are raised, and the good news is proclaimed to the poor."

Jesus wasn't concerned about what faith had brought to him or his disciples. He was concerned about what their faith was able to bring to others. That is something John would understand. John had risked his life to attack the Pharisees and Sadducees for using their faith to build their positions of wealth and power while treating those around them like they had no value. John had risked his life to stand up against the priests at the temple who took the offerings of the poor and used them for their own enrichment. John had heard all of them say that the poor, the blind, the lame, the leper, were all poor, and blind, and sick because it was God's will and they must have done something to deserve it. John understood that while the Pharisees, Sadducees, and priests looked and dressed like men of faith, their faith was misdirected and false.

As Frank's pastor visited, the pastor told him stories about all of the people whose lives had been changed because of something Frank had said or done. There was the farm family who was able to stay in their home because of the time Frank had given them more time to pay the bills they owed after a difficult year. There were the three boys who were going to be sent to jail before Frank spoke with the judge and gave them jobs at Frank's business. Those three boys ended up graduating from college and now have their own families in town. There were the many times the church had needed funds to help in an emergency, and Frank had seen to it that those funds somehow mysteriously appeared. As they talked, Frank began to smile again. He began to remember all that he had done, and why he had done it. He hadn't done those things to make sure he earned respect or gained some special benefit for himself. He had done those things because he believed it was what you did if you loved God and loved your neighbor. Frank only lived about three more months after that day the pastor visited. But those three months were filled with good times with the family, smiles each time he saw the sunrise, and a feeling of satisfaction that he had done what he could do.

I have to be honest with you here. There are still times when I struggle with this. I find myself asking that question about why Frank had to go through what he did while so many others live like Pharisees and Sadducees and don't suffer. I understand that living a faithful life means doing what we can for others, but there are times when I just get angry at how things work out. I remember people like Frank and it just bothers me.

Maybe that's why Jesus said that piece that we left off a while ago. After he told John's disciples what to tell him about, he then said, "Blessed is anyone who does not stumble on account of me." Many people skip that line, like we did, because it doesn't seem to make any sense. Why on earth would someone stumble because of Jesus? Isn't he the one that would keep us from stumbling? But I think I understand what he meant.

It is easy to live the faith of a Pharisee or Sadducee. There is comfort in knowing that if I am a good believer, good things will come to me, problems will be solved, money will come in, and when all is said and done, I will have a great reward waiting for me. There is great comfort in knowing that if I believe, I will be safe. If I believe, all is good. All I need to do is believe. That is a faith that could pick me right up and lead me through life with a smile.

Is that the faith that Jesus talks about? The faith that says that what God might do for me is not important, but what is important is what I can do for others? The faith that says it is not important to worry about what I can collect, but what is important is what I can give away? The faith that says it is not important to worry my being comfortable, but what is important is that I give comfort to others? Seriously? Give away half of what I have to the poor? Seriously? If I have two coats, give one away? Really? Those are the things that make me stumble in my faith journey. I find myself sitting in that hole with John and Frank.

But John and Frank understood. They just needed reminding. They understood that for them, their faith in God was not based on what God did for them. That was Pharisee faith. They believed that the only thing they needed to be concerned about was loving their God, and loving the people around them, plain and simple.

We give two types of gifts at Christmas time. There are those gifts we give to make sure we meet some standard that has been set. We need to make sure our gift is up to the level of the one we got from them last year, to make sure we end up looking okay. And there are those gifts we give to simply see the smile and joy in the face of the one receiving it. Not because it somehow comes back to reward us, but just because of what it means to that person getting the gift.

Just the same, there are two types of faith. The faith of the Pharisee, and the faith of John and Frank.

John's and Frank's is better.

Amen.

Advent 4

Matthew 1:18-25

# Being Different

Picture it this way. The teenage daughter walks in the house. "Hey mom, dad, guess what? I was down at the gas station filling up the car when something happened. An angel walked up and told me that I was going to have a baby. Wow! Can you believe it?"

I'm not trying to make light of the scripture today, but if you think about it, that's about how this story began. According to tradition, Mary had gone down to the village well to get water. It was one of the routine chores the young girls in the family took care of each morning. She would have carried the empty jar to the well in the center of town, filled it with water, and then lifted the heavy jar back onto her shoulder for the walk back home. But today, while she was at the well, Matthew told us an angel appeared to her with the message that she was going to have a child. God had selected her of all of the young girls in the entire world for the honor of bearing a child given her by the Holy Spirit.

We remember this story every year and smile as we think of the great things that came from Mary's role. She is remembered by many as one of the most important women in history. She is held up as a model for motherhood and a symbol of purity and faithfulness. As we experience another Christmas this week and celebrate the miracle birth, I think it is worthwhile to take a few moments and remember just what Mary experienced; what she actually went through to reach that point of honor and praise. Because, it would most certainly not have started out that way.

Many of us know what it means to live in a very small place; a small village or small neighborhood. Everyone knows everyone else and knows most of their family background as well. There is a certain comfort and security that comes with that kind of community, but there is more. There are expectations that exist; expectations of things that members of that community may and may not do. There are roles in the community, and everyone knows what everyone else's role is to be. There are rules and guidelines that define what is acceptable in the community. Those social norms exist because the place is so small and what one person does can have a real impact on everyone else in the community. One person's behavior can create a reputation that might then be associated with everyone in the community. "It's that neighborhood where…", or "It's that kind of place." There have to be rules, and those rules have to be enforced. They are not intended to be harsh or cruel, but they are seen as ways to ensure the way of life that the community has created.

While it is a large city today, Nazareth was a very small town of perhaps 300 people when Mary's family lived there. Nazareth had been around for a long time, sitting on a hill overlooking some of the most famous events of history, but is never mentioned once in the Old Testament. It was a small Jewish village. It is fairly safe to assume that when Mary went back to the well for water the next morning, well, let's just say there were some eyes following her, and a few "tisk tisks" being uttered from a few doorways. The odds are very small that the village had put up one of those banners across the street reading, "Welcome to Nazareth: Future Home of God's Own Son!"

It reminds me of another small town in one of Jesus' stories that Luke recorded. That story went something like this.

We don't know much of anything about the father and son, or what might have created the rift between them. We don't know if one of them was right and the other was wrong. We don't know if the father had been a fair man, or if the son was just rebellious. All we know is that there was a man with two sons, and one of those sons had come to dad asking him to give him his share of the estate. However tame that may sound to us today, on that day in that place, the son was essentially saying, "I've had enough. Give me what is going to be mine, and let me live my life the way I want to live it! I wish you were dead." Rather than wait for his part of the inheritance, he wanted it now. We don't know the father's thoughts as he divided things up; if he was sad, disappointed, or just relieved to see an end to the arguing, but he divided up the estate and gave his son the part that would one day have been his anyway. A few days later the boy packed up everything he owned and walked away. Out the door, down the street, out the town gate, and down the road to whatever the world was going to offer him. He was free.

As sometimes happens, the world proved to be a bit more challenging than the young man's inheritance was prepared for. He lived large for a few months, but about the time the inheritance ran out and he needed to find a job, a famine occurred making jobs scarce. Finally, the young man took a job walking fields to gather leftover grain to feed to a farmer's pigs. Pigs of all things. And they ate better than he did. Luke tells us that the young man was hungry, and that "no one gave him anything." It is the picture of loneliness. But finally, Luke says, the young man came to his senses and realized that even his father's servants were in better shape than he was. It also seems that there was more than simple hunger involved. The young man began to realize that he had hurt his father, had shamed him and needed to somehow make up for that mistake. Let's remember what happened next.

Word spread through town quickly. Someone traveling on the road had seen the young man, and he was headed in their direction. People came out of their homes and shops and headed for the town gate. Those with children brought them along because today they were going to learn a lesson that they would never forget. Today, they were going to see what happened to young men who shamed their family, and their village. Everyone knew what was going to happen. It was a law written long ago for a ceremony called the *kezazah*. The boy would walk up to the city gate. The father would stay at home and refuse to see him. Instead, villagers would meet him at the gate and throw a large clay pot on the ground at the boy's feet. The pot would shatter into pieces, representing how the relationship between the father and son was now shattered as well. The villagers would turn their backs to the boy, and the former son would turn and walk away. He would not dare enter the village he had shamed.

The village gathered at the gate and waited. When the father learned that his son was coming, the old man went to the gate. At first, people were confused, but then understood that the old man was angry and shamed enough he wanted to be there to throw the clay pot himself. This would be a lesson the village children would remember for a very long time. When the boy was seen coming toward the gate, the crowds began to shout and taunt him, encouraging the old man to teach his son a lesson and remove the shame from their village. Then the old man saw his son approaching.

Luke said, "But while he was still a long way off, his father saw him and was filled with compassion for him; he ran to his son, threw his arms around him and kissed him."

The crowd went silent. First, men do not run. To run you need to hike up your robe so you can move freely, and that means showing your legs in public. Men would not do that. It was a shameful act. And then, instead of fulfilling the *kezazah* and throwing a clay pot, the old man threw his arms around his son and kissed him, accepted his apology, and yelled to his servants to bring a clean robe, put one of his own rings on his son's finger, and put new sandals on his feet. As they walked through the town gate, the father shouted to everyone, inviting them to the big party they were having that night to celebrate his son's return. They would kill the fatted calf and everything. The old man was elated.

43

The townsfolk were in shock. They pulled their children away and sent them home. "No wonder his son behaved like he did," they said, "if that is the kind of father he has."

Not only did he run in public, and failed to perform the *kezazah*, he was treating the boy like he did nothing wrong — like he was actually happy to have him return. First, the son brought shame onto his family and his village, and now his father compounded it.

The old man did not care. We don't know how many villagers came to the party that night. All we know is that as the older son was walking back from his day of working the fields, he heard the music and dancing. He asked one of the servants what was going on. He could not believe what he heard. He stood outside the house with others from the village that were angry at the additional shame the family was bringing upon their village. The father came out and pleaded with his son to come inside and welcome his brother home, but he would have none of it. "It is not fair!" the older son said. "He brought shame on all of us. He went out and wasted everything he had living an unclean life. And now he comes crawling back, and what do you do? You bring even more shame on us. And while he's been doing all that, I've been here, working hard to support the family and village, I've followed the rules, but he's the one you throw the party for? He's the one you kill the fatted calf for?"

As the old man tried to explain, Luke left the story there, leaving us wondering how things finally worked out. Most likely it ended like this: The older son saw that he had no choice if he was going to remove the shame from his family and his village. He looked around the ground for a stone, a large stone. He picked it up and threw it at his father. Others did the same. Then they found the younger son and did the same. And finally, the shame was removed. The older brother regained the family's place in the village, and all was right with the world. We remember this story as the story of the prodigal son.

This, I am afraid, is what Mary faced as well. Her family's responsibility was clear. But even more, there was Joseph, her betrothed. This was something like a super engagement; not yet married, but more than just being engaged. They were not yet husband and wife, but if Joseph were to die, Mary would be seen as a widow. What it meant was that if Mary was going to have a child, according to the law she must have committed adultery, and the punishment was clear. At best, Joseph would beat her severely and then he and her family would send her away, carrying the reputation of an adulteress, to spend the rest of her life unmarried, alone, living on the streets as a beggar, or worse. Or, Joseph would pick up and throw the first stone, and Mary would be killed by her family and her village. That was the old law. Joseph had no choice.

We don't know much about Joseph. We don't know how he first reacted to Mary's news. We can guess how the village reacted, and the pressure they put on Joseph to act, but we don't know what was in his mind. We don't know if he was relieved when the angel appeared to him to confirm what Mary said, or if it was still difficult for him to get past the feeling that he had been shamed. What we do know is that somehow, Joseph and Mary found the strength to stand together and believe together that they were doing something that was bigger than the old laws.

They were doing something that was more important than the stares and jeers they would have faced every day from the people who did not understand.

As we go through our week of Christmas this week, and as we meet all of the people whose paths we are going to cross… let us remember… we are to be different.

Remember the young couple in Nazareth. This week we sing about them as people whom God honored and blessed. Back then, everyone whispered about them as shameful people who no longer had value or a rightful place in the community.

Remember that our role is not to determine the value of those around us and decide whether or not we think they are a risk to what we believe is right and just. Our role is to love our God, and love those other people who are around us - not just family or those who behave like we do. We are to love all of them, even the Mary and Josephs. We are to be different.

That's the gift that Mary offers us this week.

Merry Christmas.

Amen.

Christmas Day/Eve

Luke 2:1-14, (15-20)

# Ponder This!

This is the story we remember. There is Mary and Joseph, the animals, the shepherds, the angels, and the baby all wrapped up and lying in a manger. It is quiet and calm. The star is floating overhead. Even the animals seem to understand that something important has happened. This is the image of Christmas the artists recreate, and the Christmas we show every year with our nativity scenes.

As I remember the story now and think of that image of all of them gathered around the little baby, I find one line from the scripture kind of sticking in my mind more than the rest. It's that line I've heard over and over, but haven't really paid much attention to it because it really just doesn't sound all that important considering all the rest. It is the line that says, "But Mary treasured up all these things and pondered them in her heart." Especially that last part where Mary "pondered them in her heart."

I looked up that word; ponder. The dictionary says that to ponder means to "think about (something) carefully, especially before making a decision or reaching a conclusion." Another one says to ponder means "to spend time thinking carefully and seriously about a problem or a difficult question." And it just strikes me strange, that in the middle of this wonderful image of peacefulness and calm, Mary is pondering. It seems like she would be relieved, and tired, and just kind of chilling out. But Luke says she was pondering, thinking seriously about some problem or difficult question; some type of decision that had to be made. Mary was pondering. It just seems out of place.

Until I remember the full story.

Then I imagine that part of what Mary is pondering is what happened back in Nazareth after the angel had first told her she was going to have the baby. The things said to her by people in town, and most of all, the look on Joseph's face when she first told him. She was grateful that the angel had finally explained things to him, but until that happened it had been difficult, to say the least. Then the people talked about Joseph too, and how he had allowed her to shame them like she did.

And when they found out about the census and the long trip they had to take to Jerusalem, the difficulties of the trip were almost seen as a welcomed relief to just get them out of town for a while, away from the criticism and shaming.

But the journey was a long walk, more than 100 miles along roads and paths through really difficult territory. And it was a walk. Mary and Joseph were not wealthy. We know that because after the baby was born and they went to the temple to give their offering, we're told they gave two doves or two pigeons. That is the offering of the poor, not the well-to-do. They would not have had a donkey for Mary to ride to Jerusalem, so they walked.

There were two usual ways to get from Nazareth to Jerusalem, neither was easy. You could travel east to the Sea of Galilee, and then go south along the Jordan River valley. It was rugged land bordering the wilderness, a very difficult journey for a young woman expecting a child. The other route was just straight south through the high country. The roads were better, but it could be cold there, and the path went through Samaria. The Jews and the Samaritans had been at odds ever since the Babylonian exile. It may have been generations ago, but the feelings were still very much alive. While Mary and Joseph could have traveled the roads through Samaria, they would have had to dodge the sticks and stones that would have been thrown at them along the way. Regardless of what their son would say years later, Mary and Joseph both knew very well there was no such thing as a "good" Samaritan.

And, whichever route they took, the roads would have been crowded with other travelers. Everyone in the land was to return to their place of birth to be counted in the census. The roads were crowded. Mary and Joseph walked and tried to stay out of the way of the well-to-do with their carts and wagons hogging the road. The wagon-riders also had the advantage of not having to deal with the beggars. The roads filled with travelers attracted every kind of beggar from throughout the land. Mary and Joseph would have been constantly approached by those with their hands out...the lame, the blind, the lepers. According to the laws, a woman bearing a child who is touched by the unclean should immediately bathe herself or risk becoming unclean herself. But there were no ritual bath-houses along the roads. Joseph did his best to protect her, but the roads were crowded.

And as they passed through the city of Jerusalem and neared Bethlehem, the crowds became even larger. If there were rooms available, they were only for those who could pay the high prices the landlords knew they could get during the census. Price gouging is not a new thing. Nor are pickpockets, and scam artists. Crowds coming in from every small village in the country presented a great opportunity for city-wise criminals. Even if you might find an available room, it might be nothing more than a ruse to get you away from the crowds where you could be robbed in private.

Finally, we are told that one homeowner saw Mary and the look on her face, and took pity on them. Or, some traditions say they finally found the home of a relative, and even though the place was already over-crowded, family hospitality was honored. Either way, Mary and Joseph were led through the front part of the house built against the hill, into the cave in the back of the house where the animals were kept. Whatever else you might say about the place, the smells, and the animals, at least it was out of the crowds. We don't know how long Mary and Joseph were there, but at some point, the baby was born. He was wrapped in cloth, and placed in one of the large, stone feeding troughs separating the cave-room from the rest of the house.

Then the shepherds arrived. They talked about angels and the baby. The shepherds were excited and told everyone they saw about the baby. Word spread and the crowds began to gather. People came to see the miracle baby. At one point, three foreign men came in. They were wealthy men, carrying gifts for the baby. Mary watched as one of the men placed pieces of gold next to the baby. Another placed a jar of frankincense. The third a jar of myrrh. These were gifts usually presented at the birth of a king. They were also gifts typically used for embalming.

Mary watched, and treasured up all these things and pondered them in her heart. She pondered. I wonder if she was thinking about the honor of being the mother of a king, or if she was just trying to think of how to protect her newborn baby boy? I wonder if she was trying to decide what kinds of things she needed to do to raise her son as God intended, or if she was trying to come up with a way to just make all of this go away so she could be a mother to her son. I wonder if she was calm and at ease inside, or if she was terrified and trying to find some way to grab her baby, get out of town, and go someplace where no one knew who they were? The artists seem to believe she was doing just fine, and show her face as one of peace and assurance. But I wonder.

Please understand. I am not trying to ruin this wonderful image or pull the rug out from under your Christmas. And I am not at all trying to lessen the image of Mary. All I am wondering if Mary might have been different than the image we often see of her, and just a bit more like you and me? If even in the middle of what she had been told was something from God, if even then she might have wondered... might have questioned... might

51

have pondered… like I would have? Because if she did… if she did have questions or doubts… even brief ones… she was still able to find a way to do what needed to be done.

For me, if she could do that… be human and have human questions… and still, find the strength to do what God wanted her to do… then she reminds me today that there may still be hope for me as well. And that, for me, is the true miracle of Christmas.

Merry Christmas.

Amen.

Christmas 1

Matthew 2:13-23

# After Everyone Had Gone Home

It was over. The shepherds had gone back to their flocks. The three wise men had gone to wherever they were going, the other visitors that had come to see what was going on had drifted away to other things, and the animals had begun to settle back down in the straw. Mary was resting and the baby was sleeping soundly. Joseph looked around the room and let out a long, deep breath. "It was over." He leaned back against the wall and closed his eyes, looking forward to a much-needed long night's sleep.

Then the angel showed up.

We come together here after our week of celebrating one of the central holidays of our faith. And, as we gather, many of us have one key thought running through our minds.

"It is over! We survived another one!"

Although this is a joyous season of celebration in the life of the church, for many of us it is also a long line of days filled with stress and pressures, with full schedules and full houses. For others, it can be quiet, sometimes too quiet. With the stresses coming from too-full schedules or too-empty houses, some of us may have come here now looking for some words of assurance; some words of joy and happiness to remind us of the true meaning of the season.

But instead, we read one of the most difficult and painful passages in the entire Bible. Matthew reminds us of what followed that first Christmas celebration, and at least for me, it's not the kind of message I was looking for today. Instead of remembering the angels and shepherds, the gifts and the baby, we are reminded that there are people in this world who do unimaginably cruel things to get what they want.

According to the story, when the wise men came from across the desert to find the baby, word of their arrival got to King Herod. Not much slipped-passed Herod. He immediately scheduled a reception for the foreign dignitaries, and at some point during the formal dinner he pulled the three aside and spoke with them. He told them how honored he was to have them travel so far to visit his land, and how excited he was for them to find the baby they had come to find. Herod knew how to play an audience, even a small one. He asked them to do him a personal favor. When they finally found the baby they were looking for, would they please send him a message and tell him where that baby was... so he could also come and pay his respects. Fortunately, the three men were called "wise" for a reason and easily saw through Herod's act. After presenting their gifts to the baby, Matthew said they "departed to their own country by another way." They ignored Herod's favor and just went home.

Anyone who knew King Herod knew there were two things you never did. First, you never did anything that might give him the idea that you might be a threat to his role as king. Second, you never skipped out when Herod asked you for a favor. So, Herod was already upset about this new baby many were saying would grow up and become a king. When he learned that the three men had found that baby but had then taken off, Herod was furious.

He called the chief priests and scribes from the temple and asked them what they knew about this new baby-king. They quoted a passage from the scroll of Micah saying that one day a ruler would come from the town of Bethlehem. That was all Herod needed to hear.

Herod knew how to deal with threats to his control. One day someone had mentioned to him how quickly the king's son was growing, and how strong of a man he would soon be. Herod said, "Thank you" and sent a few guys down the hall to kill that his son. Herod's favorite wife Miriamne gave him two sons who were recognized as strong and brave children. Herod invited them to go swimming with him in the palace swimming pool, where he drowned them both. Eventually, he also murdered his favorite wife, Miriamne, her brother, her grandfather, her mother, some 45 members of the Sanhedrin, and hundreds of friends and family members, give or take a dozen or two. The historian Augustus once said, "It was better to be Herod's pig than than Herod's son." Herod knew how to deal with threats to his control.

He sent a few messages, made a few calls, tweeted a few tweets, and a couple of nights later a group of his most loyal supporters showed up in Bethlehem. They did not go quietly, sneaking down dark alleyways, but marched through the main streets of town carrying torches and waving banners, shouting to every household to watch and learn what happens to anyone who dares to challenge the authority of the king. We aren't exactly sure just how long after the actual birth of the baby this happened, and apparently, Herod wasn't either, because the mob entered every house and killed every male child under the age of two. Herod was not taking any chances. Herod knew how to deal with threats to his control.

Before we go further, looking back on this scene, some people try to point out a few positive things about what Herod's mob did that night in Bethlehem. First, at the time it happened, Bethlehem was a rather small town. They remind us that there were probably only thirty to 35 male children under the age of two in the village that night. But, you know, somehow I don't think that makes much difference to those thirty or 35 families.

Second, even Matthew points out that Herod's actions were clearly fulfilling a prophecy from Jeremiah, giving even more evidence that the baby Jesus was the long-awaited Messiah. But again, I'm thinking that wasn't all that much of a comfort for those families visited by Herod's mobs.

And third, the fact that when the mob made their attack in Bethlehem, Mary, Joseph, and the baby were already well on their way to safety in Egypt because of that dream Joseph had. That dream saved them and kept the new king safe. It was a miracle dream. But, if I was one of the fathers in Bethlehem burying my son, I honestly don't think that's the miracle I would be much interested in hearing.

Whatever we do take from this frightening story, it is a classic example of someone who represented everything that Jesus would later stand and speak against. If we wanted to find a good example of the meaning of "evil", of the opposite of what Christmas represents, King Herod might be enough.

With that said, I need to take just a few minutes to say something else. As I remember this story today, I have to admit that I feel sorry for King Herod. I'm not trying to make less of the things he did in his life, or somehow excuse his behavior, but standing here this close to Christmas, I can't help but feel sorry for him.

In some ways, he never had a chance. He was at fault, made absolutely wrong choices, but he was groomed for that, and he was surrounded by people who benefited from his behaviors. Herod's power made other people wealthy, made them "right," and those people did everything they could do to encourage him to keep it up. And as long as they bowed and agreed at the right times, Herod rewarded their loyalty by making them wealthy and allowing them to enjoy their control. The leaders back in Rome loved him because he kept the country under control. They didn't care how he did it, as long as he did it. Herod was wrong, but he was also created and enabled. It is far too simple to stand here and point a finger and say, "Bad Herod!" It was far too simple then, and now. What evil we may face today is, in part, because of decisions and choices made by our parents. What evil our children will face in their future is, in part, because of decisions you and I are making today. I feel sorry for Herod because, whatever else he was, he was a pawn in a game. He was being used.

I also feel sorry for Herod because he was so alone. I have never met anyone as alone and lonely as the men and women I have met in positions of great control. Oh, they don't look lonely, that's for sure. They are busy, have the benefits and toys that come with control, but they spend their days and nights living inside a bubble. It is a bubble that protects them from the things that might threaten their control. Only rarely does any other person get inside that bubble. The person in control is always surrounded by others, but those others are there because of the control, not the person. Some of those people gain from being close, some are hoping to someday get some pieces of the control for themselves, but very few are there because they simply want to be there. Even fewer are there because they truly love and care for the person inside the bubble. I feel sorry for Herod because there was he was alone, fully and truly alone. No one cared.

And, I feel sorry for Herod because he did not understand that control is always temporary; always changing. No matter how many he killed or how many mobs he sent out, there was no possible way for him to protect his control. The point was coming when it would be gone. Herod feared losing control. That meant that he awoke every morning fearing what the day might bring. Today we talk about control as like a pendulum; it first swings one way, and then the other. We talk about what we will do when we regain control or we talk about the things we must do to keep them from getting control. We focus on holding tightly to something of which we can never keep hold. That leads to an endless loop of mornings that bring new threats until we are finally faced with the reality that controllers always eventually lose.

I feel sorry for Herod. He lived a life of loneliness that he constantly tried to fill. He possessed things, killed threats, and ended up spending his final years alone, spending every day lying in ice water to ease the pain from the diseases that came from his years of pleasure-seeking. Shortly before he died, he once again sent his mobs to round up dozens of respected men from around the country and had them brought to his temple in Jericho. He ordered that when he died, those men were to be killed as well to make sure that someone wept during his funeral. And after he died, he is remembered not as a great leader or a god, but as an example of complete corruptness and failure as a human being.

There is an attraction to being in control. A promise of power, of security, of being right. None of us are immune from it, even the church itself. We all know what it feels like to have no power, to have no security, to be accused of always being wrong. Control looks so good. Control looks like an answer. It looks like the solution to our problems.

But based on the story of the Christmas baby, we were never called to be in control. We were never called to be powerful. We were never called to be right. Those are the concerns of the Sadducees, the Pharisees, and kings like Herod. We are called to be something different.

As trite or "weak" as it sounds, we are called to love. We are called to not wake up every morning wondering how we are going to protect ourselves from those trying to take our control away, but we are to wake up wondering how we can care for others today.

That does not mean that we simply sit back and say or do nothing when control is being misused around us. We can speak up, we can take roles that give us the ability to participate in leadership. But whatever we do, we do not do it to gain or keep control. We do it because our role is to do what we believe shows love for others. And while that seems so trite and simple, it is the most difficult thing we are ever asked to do.

Amen.

John 1: (1-9), 10-18

# Other People's Mail

As we hear the Christmas story told by the writer of the gospel of John, one thought may be going through your mind:

"What the heck is that?"

What is: *"In the beginning was the Word, and the Word was with God, and the Word was God. He was with God in the beginning. Through him all things were made; without him nothing was made that has been made."*

What happened to: *"In those days a decree when out from Caesar Augustus that all the world should be taxed..."*

Sometimes, it sounds like John is writing a paper for a seminary theology class instead of telling the stories that Matthew, Mark, and Luke told. They talked about dreams, angels, and shepherds, and John talked about...well, what the heck was John talking about? The Christmas story sounds so simple until John showed up. Why was it so different?

And, while we're asking questions, sometimes Matthew, Mark, Luke, and John even seem to be telling different versions of the same story. When Jesus was baptized, one book said that John recognized Jesus when he walked up, but another one said he didn't recognize him. One book said that Jesus heard God speak after he was baptized. Another book said John heard God, and the third one said that everyone there heard God's voice. Why are they different? What the heck am I really supposed to believe here?

If this sounds like you, first of all, don't feel bad; you're not alone. And second, it is not wrong to ask these questions. The idea that we should not seriously study and ever ask questions about the Bible is a relatively new idea. It started in the last hundred years or so as people began to fear that science was becoming a threat to true faith. Rather than try to understand how they might support each other, these people decided to kind of lock the Bible up and say that anyone who questioned anything written in it was wrong. Before that, even Thomas Jefferson had enough questions about what he read in the Bible that he rewrote parts of it, and we have what is called the Jeffersonian Bible. So, questioning does not mean a lack of faith. In fact, honest questioning can lead to strengthening our faith. Maybe we can take that approach here today.

John does write differently than the other three writers. And, yes, they sometimes tell different versions of the same stories; sometimes very different. But let's see if we can understand why that is true, and see if asking questions about those differences threatens our faith, or strengthens it. I promise I'll do my best to keep this from sounding too much like one of those seminary classrooms.

Let me begin by reading something that does not come from the Bible, but something that might help us get started. How many here have bought a new phone and then had to spend some time figuring out how to use the thing? I have here a set of written instructions from the telephone company explaining how to use your new telephone. Let's go through them.

> Remove the handset from the cradle.
> Place the headset next to your ear and listen for a dial tone.
> Place your finger on the first number you wish to dial.
> Rotate the dial clockwise until your finger touches the metal stop.
> Remove your finger from the opening.
> Find the second number and repeat steps three through five.
> Return the phone to the cradle when you are finished with your conversation.

Is there a problem with those instructions? They don't work? Well, are they wrong? Is there something incorrect about them? No. They are the correct steps to follow to use your new telephone anytime between 1919 and around 1980 when the rotary dial phone began to be replaced by the push-button phone. It is confusing today, but it is not wrong. They are simply instructions written for another time.

That is something very important for us to keep in mind as we read the gospels, in fact, when we read the entire Bible. We sometimes think the writers of the Bible were writing a history book or creating a record for us to read here today some two or three thousand years later. But those writers did not have us in mind as they wrote. They had something far more important to do. They had a message to communicate to their readers.

Let's look at just one word for a moment. As many of the early writings were passed around they were called by the Greek word *euaggelizo*, which meant "the good message." Years later, in Old English, that word ended up becoming "godspel," which meant "glad tidings." The words both meant the same thing but were words used to make the most sense to the people of that day. The writers had an important message to present, and they wanted to make sure that message was understood.

Remember, the message is always the same; just the words are changed to make sure that message is understood. Now, let's get our hands dirty.

The book of Mark was the first book written, probably sometime between the years 70 and 75 AD. Let's think about who Mark was writing to. Perhaps most importantly, Mark was writing for some people who remembered Jesus when he was living with them and who were still trying to follow his teachings. Others may not have been born yet when Jesus was there, but they had joined the other believers and became a part of the early church. But that was not a good place to be right now. In the year 66, the Jews from Judea had started a full-scale revolt against the Romans. They lost. To demonstrate their victory, in the year 70 the Romans marched into Jerusalem and completely destroyed the four-hundred-year-old temple, the center of Judaism. Historians say the Romans did such a good job that they left no stones larger than a grapefruit. The destruction was total, as was the pressure then put upon all Jews and early Christians to conform to Roman control. Mark is writing to the members of that small, new bunch of Christians who are being told to either give up their faith, or die.

Mark's message is brief and may be best shown in the story of Jesus' arrest. Mark said that when Jesus went to Gethsemane, he told his disciples how sorrowful he felt, and then stepped away and fell on the ground in prayer. When he came back everyone was asleep. Jesus was fully alone. Judas then arrived with a small group of thugs from the chief priests and scribes, and after a brief confrontation, the disciples all took off, leaving Jesus to be dragged away. Mark writes his story of Gethsemane as a lesson on how to die in the faith. However alone and frightened Jesus may have felt, he held to his faith. That is what it is like to die like Jesus. All of Mark's writings were written to have meaning for this group of followers, not just for us.

The next book written was Matthew, sometime between the years 75 and 85. Matthew was sharing the same good message, but he was writing to the community he lived in, which was the Jewish community. Matthew told many of the same stories but makes it a point to repeatedly compare Jesus with Moses, the key figure of the Jewish faith. For Matthew, Jesus was the new Moses. Jesus preached his sermon from the mountain, just like Moses. Jesus not only talked about the laws of Moses, but he said he had come to fulfill them. Matthew's audience was concerned about the laws, who enforced the laws, and what happened to those to violated the laws. Matthew wrote to have meaning for his Jewish community, not just for us.

Luke was the third book written, sometime between the years 80 and 90. Luke may have been a physician, and he wrote his material for his community of well-educated people. Most importantly, his community was gentile, not Jewish. Jewish laws were of less importance. Education and wisdom were valued here, along with justice. So more than the others, Luke told his parables and stories, all with strong messages about justice and true righteousness. While it would have been difficult to find anyone in a town like Nazareth who could even read, from his earliest days Jesus walked into the synagogue and read the old scrolls of Isaiah. Later he stood on the steps of the temple itself and argued down the wisest theologians of the land. He was a Jewish scholar; a teacher with insight and true wisdom. Luke wrote to have meaning for his educated, Gentile community, not just for us.

And then came John. We believe John was written sometime around the year 95, but it could have been later. More importantly, John was writing to his community of Jewish-Christians who were living far away in the land of the Gentiles. He was writing to a small group of Christians who still felt a connection with their Jewish beginnings, but were being marginalized. Not only did their former Jewish community no longer accept them, but they were living in a land where they were having to compete with countless other religions, all of which had more strength and control. Every street corner had a different temple on it, and each of those temples offered a faith that looked to be a lot more fun than what John's followers offered. John was writing to a community under pressure; a community that was being pushed to their limits. They were hanging on by their fingernails and were growing increasingly frustrated and angry. John was writing to have meaning for his community there, not just for us.

To understand John, let's look again at the story about Jesus being arrested. Mark told us that Judas arrived with a group of thugs from the temple to get Jesus. In John's story, Judas showed up with a full cohort of Roman soldiers; that's 600 armed Centurions. And while Mark told us that Jesus fell to the ground in despair, John tells us that it was those 600 Centurions who fell to the ground in fear when Jesus spoke to them. John was writing to a church under attack, and they needed to hear about a Jesus who offered them the power and strength to stand strong. The angrier they became, the more that anger was reflected in John's writing to them. When Mark wrote about Jesus being arrested he said that the crowd was against him. When Matthew wrote about it he said the people were against him. When John wrote about it he said the Jews were against Jesus. The enemy became bigger as the communities faced more pressures.

This points out one very dangerous point of not looking closely at the writings, and not understanding who they were written for, and why. At times John said very strong things against the Jews, although everyone understood he was talking specifically about those Jews who were fighting against the new Christians. John even compared those Jews to the devil. Many years later as the Christian world grew into power, some people used John's words as the excuse to brand the entire community of Jews of that day as evil, branding them as agents of the devil and working to destroy them. That is not what John was saying when he wrote those words, but his words were misunderstood and misused. There is a real danger in insisting that we understand things that we do not truly understand.

But, if the writers of the Bible wrote different things, what can we believe? Who was right and who was wrong? Did Jesus fall down or did the soldiers? Did John recognize Jesus or did he not recognize him? Did just Jesus hear God's voice or John's, or did everyone hear it? If the stories are all different, what are we supposed to believe?

I find an answer in the words we read from John's gospel today. John was writing to a church that was overwhelmed with questions. And, since he was writing to Greeks who understood philosophy, he used philosophical language to make sure they understood the good message. He used the Greek word *logos*, which we interpret as "word." But *logos* is bigger than that. It isn't talking about a group of letters strung together to form a word. *Logos* is the essence of, or the heartfelt meaning of that word. *Logos* is the source of energy behind the word, the power that the word attempts to describe. John was writing to his community to tell them that the source of all things in the entire creation is God. God is the *logos*; the source of it all. And that source became flesh and walked around among us, even though most never recognized it. We sometimes get all tied up worrying about words, and miss the meaning they were meant to communicate. If you want to be a part of that eternal power that is God, all you need to do is look at the way Jesus lived and follow the same guidelines:

Where there is darkness, shine a light.

Seek to serve, not to control.

Our responsibility is to love God and love those around us. No more, and no less.

In my imagination, as I think of the image of walking up to a gate and facing a list of questions from an angel in charge of admissions, I can't imagine that angel asking me if I can tell him exactly how many people showed up to arrest Jesus that night. And I can't imagine that angel asking who fell down on the ground, Jesus or the soldiers? But you know, I can imagine that angel looking me right in the eyes and asking, Did you love God? And, did you love your neighbor?

That is the message I hear communicated to every community addressed by the gospels. That is the *logos*... the good message.

Amen.

Baptism of the Lord

Matthew 3:13-17

# Imagine This!

We're going to start the story today some 400 miles away from the Jordan River. The city of Tarsus was a major business center in what is now Turkey and a place where many Jewish families had settled who had fled the harsh Roman rule around Jerusalem. We're going to start by looking at one particular Jewish family in Tarsus. It was a devout Jewish family. A son in that family would later refer to himself as "of the stock of Israel, of the tribe of Benjamin, a Hebrew of the Hebrews; as touching the law, a Pharisee." This son, whose name was Saul, was proud of that heritage, and when he was old enough his family sent him all the way to Jerusalem to study the law, to continue his family's proud tradition.

Saul's family must have had some clout because Saul's teacher was a man called Gamaliel, still recognized as one of the most respected teachers in the land. Gamaliel was the grandson of Hillel the Elder, one of the most important men in Jewish history. Hillel the Elder was involved in developing the Talmud and Mishnah, two of the most important books in the Jewish tradition. Gamaliel was considered to be a doctor of Jewish law and was a very powerful Pharisee. There was a group of seventy-one teachers that made up a group called the Sanhedrin; the supreme court of the day. Gamaliel was on the Sanhedrin, and for a while may have been the head of that powerful body. To become one of Gamaliel's students was quite a deal and was an almost guaranteed pathway to position and power in the Jewish community.

We aren't told anything about Saul's experience as Gamaliel's student. All we have is a note from one historian who described one of Gamaliel's students who displayed "impudence in learning." Based on what we do know about Saul, it's not difficult to imagine that this historian was talking about him. A young man from a proud family with the right lineage and the resources to send him all the way to the temple to the most important teacher in the land; yes, this just might be Saul the historian was talking about.

We know that at some point, Saul progressed well enough in his studies to officially and formally become a Pharisee, following his family heritage. He would have spent years studying the Jewish laws, learning all of their interpretations. It's just my imagination, but I can see this proud young man wearing his Pharisaic robes, honing his skills by arguing the intricacies of the laws with the other students, feeling the importance of his role as the one carrying on the traditions of his ancestors. I can imagine he might have been a bit impudent at times, even arguing with his teachers about some finer points of the various laws. In my mind, he could be a bit cocky, sure of himself, convinced that it was his responsibility to defend and enforce the laws to the absolute best of his ability. And, in my imagination, that is what led him to make the trip down to the Jordan River that morning to evaluate the rumors of a possible new threat there.

Remember, this is just my imagination talking here now. There is nothing written to support this part of my story. But, to me, it seems like something that could have happened, and it helps me understand what is to come later.

As I hear the words from Matthew today, I can see John standing out in the middle of the Jordan River, just as he had done for a while. But today, Jesus is standing out there with him, his hair still wet from the water John had just poured over his head. Along both sides of the river, I see the crowds. They have come from all over the place to see John, and many had come to be baptized themselves because of their belief in John's message. But right now, they are all very quiet. Something has happened they are having a difficult time understanding. After John had poured the water over Jesus' head, there was a sound. Some thought it was a rush of wind in the trees, some thought it was thunder, while others would swear it was an actual voice. They all looked at John hoping he would explain what was going on. John was just staring at Jesus. John realized that something very important had just happened.

And over there on the riverbank, Saul had been sitting on a rock watching John do his thing. But now Saul is standing, his eyes narrow and his head cocked to one side to try and hear everything that was going on. Saul realized that something important had just happened too. This little prophet and his sideshow had just become something much bigger. He couldn't wait to get back to the temple and tell Gamaliel. This was what he had spent all those years studying for.

As the story continues in my mind, by the time Saul got back to Jerusalem he had prepared his argument for what had to be done about this threat growing at the Jordan River. He could specify the laws that explained the threats John and this Jesus were creating, as well as the specific punishments for each of those violations. As the impudent student Pharisee, I wonder if Saul was even a bit excited, seeing this as his big chance. Some of the other students had laughed at him for making the long trip to the river just to see another of the long list of crack-pot, self-proclaimed prophets. But now, Saul had his opportunity to not only make them pay for their laughter but show everyone just how good of a Pharisee he was going to be.

I believe Saul was disappointed. As he presented his case to his teacher, Gamaliel seemed to not share his concern. Saul repeated the account of what he saw and heard. Gamaliel nodded but did not offer the praise and pat-on-the-back that Saul had expected. Saul was confused.

It wasn't that Saul hadn't made a good case, or that Gamaliel did not understand or believe what Saul told him. But if though he was a Pharisee with an even more impressive lineage than Saul, Gamaliel looked at things a bit differently.

While putting Saul at the Jordan River is just my imagination, historians do give us a clear picture of how Gamaliel would probably have responded to Saul's report. A few years later some of the apostles were arrested and brought before the Sanhedrin for trial. The group wanted to make an example of these men and demanded that they all be immediately put to death. Then Gamaliel spoke. He began by reminding them of Theudas and Judas, two other self-proclaimed prophets who had risen up in recent years. Both of those men drew a crowd for a while, but after a few months the crowds drifted away and the prophets when back to their day jobs. Gamaliel said, "And now I say unto you, refrain from these men, and let them alone: for if this counsel or this work be of men, it will come to naught: But if it be of God, ye cannot overthrow it; lest haply ye be found even to fight against God."

The Sanhedrin was convinced, but in my imagination, Saul was not. Saul was more confused than convinced. How could this man, this teacher, this Pharisee, allow this type of threat to continue? How could a man so devoted to the laws of Moses stand aside and allow a group to so blatantly say things that go against those sacred laws? The fire that had already burned inside the impudent student had begun to burn as something much, much hotter.

The historians do give us another glimpse into the life of the young Pharisee Saul as his role as a Pharisee grew. Not long after Jesus was crucified, a disciple named Stephen was arrested and brought to Jerusalem for trial. Apparently, there was now enough noise being made by Jesus followers that the Sanhedrin was not as flexible as they had been before. The decision was made that Stephen should be killed by stoning to make a powerful point. Stephen would have been taken to one of the gates of the city as the law prescribes. To keep it from getting completely out of control, one Pharisee would have been put in charge of the proceedings. This was a position of honor, given to the Pharisee who best represented the laws of Moses and their meanings. As the crowds gathered, they would each take off their robe and put it at the feet of the Pharisee in charge, then pick up a stone and throw it. It was as brutal as you can imagine. And, the historians tell us, standing there with a look of pride and justice in his eyes, with his feet surrounded by the robes of the stone-throwers, was Saul.

The fire inside of Saul had begun to burn even hotter as he hunted for more of these Christians of which to make examples. I can imagine Gamaliel trying to speak with his former student, urging him to reconsider, but the impudent student was now the impudent Pharisee who was dedicated to his role as protector of the laws. The Sanhedrin gave Saul and his followers authority to go from town to town, hunting down Christians and standing at city gates with their shoes covered in robes. He was good at what he did and proud to be serving his faith. But, as I imagine the story, somewhere in the places we only hear during the quietness of the nighttime, Saul struggled with his thoughts about his old teacher. He could not understand why this man of such learning and understanding was not out here with him, bringing these enemies of the faith to justice. It made no sense in his Saul's mind.

But what happened next was just too much.

Saul had done such a good job of Christian-hunting that many had left the country to find safety elsewhere, like the Syrian city of Damascus. Eventually, the Sanhedrin gave him permission to go there as well, so Saul began the trip north to the Damascus road.

Once again, in my mind, one morning on that journey a someone from the temple arrived with the message that Gamaliel and two of his sons had converted. Gamaliel, the Pharisee of Pharisees, the greatest teacher of the law ever known, had now become a Christian. That part is true. Gamaliel and his sons did become Christian. The only part we are imagining is how Saul found out. But in that imagining, can you see Saul's face? I see a flash of doubt, then confusion, and then a growing anger. I wonder if Gamaliel and the boys had gone to Damascus? I wonder....

All we know is that the Road to Damascus follows a path around the edge of Mount Hermon, a place known for quick weather changes, winds, and storms. We're told that at some point along that stretch of road, something changed in Saul. It is described as one of those miracles in which God suddenly interrupts human history, using raw power to make needed changes. That story says that as Saul traveled past the mountain, there was a huge flash of light and Saul fell from his horse. He heard a voice from heaven saying "Saul, why are you persecuting me?" The result was that Saul, the Pharisee, became Paul, the disciple.

I'm not trying to deny that story, but back in that world of my imagination, I wonder if God might have taken a different approach. I wonder if God had kept Saul lying awake over the past few nights trying to make sense of what Gamaliel had said and done? I wonder if, as certain as Saul was about his work, Gamaliel had somehow caused Saul to wonder. I wonder if Saul had awoken that morning, looked up at the heavens that had given him the laws, and said something like, "Come on God, give me some kind of sign here. I thought it was our responsibility to show how powerful our laws are, not to be weak and let people walk all over them. Why don't you say something?"

Then God said something. It doesn't matter to me if there was a heavenly flash or just one of those normal mountainside storms, and it doesn't matter to me if there was a voice or just one of those really deep and low rumbles that shakes your very bones.

I like that better because it gives me more hope. It reminds me that I don't have to look for those miracles to make things change. I'd like to think it wasn't a miraculous bolt thrown by an angel that converted Saul but was the actions of the old man Gamaliel that finally removed the scales from Saul's eyes. I like it better if, instead of God intervening with a miracle, God just used Gamaliel kept bugging Saul until he finally came to realize the truth. Because if that's true, then maybe God will find ways to use me some time as well.

Saul finished his trip to Damascus, but instead of standing at the city gate holding robes, he went into hiding to avoid the other groups of Christian-hunters he had himself created. He avoided them for a long time. He avoided them long enough to travel throughout Asia, and some say even as far as Spain. He avoided them long enough to write letters to other Christians, encouraging them and teaching them. He even returned to Jerusalem four times to support the Christians there. He had become popular enough that the Sanhedrin was afraid to arrest him—until he went back the fifth time. This time, the Sanhedrin had prepared for him. They found a group of people from Asia who would testify that Paul was breaking the laws of Moses by telling people they did not have to be circumcised. During that fifth trip, Paul was arrested and dragged before the Sanhedrin. He would have recognized many faces. The decision was a quick one, and the robe-holding Pharisee was selected to manage the stoning. Then Paul spoke.

Saul was Jewish, but he had been born in Tarsus. That made him officially a Roman. Any Roman who was accused of a crime had the right to ask for a one-on-one hearing with Caesar himself. Paul asked for that and the Sanhedrin had no choice. Paul was placed under house arrest until he was shipped off to Rome. He remained prisoner there for two more years before he had his hearing. Some historians say it was Emperor Nero himself that beheaded Paul. Saul was born a Pharisee, the son of Pharisees, the protector of the laws of Moses. Paul died as a man many believed did more than any other person in history to support and expand the Christian faith.

It is a powerful story about the changes that are possible in our lives. Most all of what we have talked about is historical, except the place we began, with Saul making that trip to the Jordan River. But as I look back at all that was to happen, I can really imagine; John in the river... Jesus standing next to him... a voice from heaven... Saul standing next to a tree shaking his head. I can see it.

It gives me hope.

Amen.

# What About Me?

The scripture today is another one of those interesting passages from John, this time giving us John's version of the story about Jesus being baptized. The other gospel writers tell the story in fairly clear ways, describing what Jesus and John said and did. After reading their stories, we can close our eyes and see what it must have been like.

And then John writes his version and instead of telling us about the river, he says things like, "This is the man I told you about who comes after me and would end up going past me because he had already been here before me the entire time." And suddenly, the image of the two guys standing in the middle of the river with a dove flying over their heads turns into a "HUH?"

But to be honest with you, that line doesn't really bother me all that much. I remember that John was writing his stories for people who were a part of the Greek culture, and I remember that John's more flowery, philosophical language was what they were used to. So it really isn't a big problem if I don't fully understand what John is writing here; he didn't write it for me. We are reading someone else's mail here, and what is important is that those people understood it, not us. We'll stick with the other three writers who wrote to people more like us.

So I'm not bothered that much by things John wrote here that I'm not sure I fully understand. What bothers is are some of the things he wrote here that I think I really do understand. Those are the lines I'm thinking about today.

I'm thinking about the line that says that John the Baptist was there again, and two of his disciples were there with him. This was after Jesus had been baptized and things happened to make it pretty clear that Jesus was the Messiah, not John. So, I'm thinking about those disciples of John who apparently didn't make the switch. For whatever reason, they stayed with John instead of moving over to Jesus' team. It just reminds me of how hard it sometimes is for me to change, even when I know full well I really should do it. Maybe they stayed out of simple loyalty. Maybe they stayed because they were familiar with John and it was more comfortable to just stay put. Maybe they had a role or position of importance with John, and going with Jesus would mean giving that up and having to start all over again. Maybe they just didn't want to change. I can understand all of those. It makes them all a bit more human to me. That means even people like me may be able to end up doing something meaningful like they ended up doing.

Apparently, John and his two disciples saw Jesus passing by and when John pointed him out his two disciples went over to Jesus to kind of check him out. At some point, John tells us that Jesus turned around and looked at them and said, "What do you want?"

That line kind of blows my mind. Can you imagine? Think about it for a moment. Imagine that Jesus looked you right in the eyes and asked, "What do you want?" What would you say?

Answers? Do you want answers to some questions that have bothered you for a really long time? Why did she have to get so sick and die so young? Why did things fall apart like they did? Why is life so difficult? Why do good people suffer and bad people...?" or maybe, "Should we follow you now or stay with John?" You know the list. It seems like we all have one, and there are those times when we would just like to have a few of those questions answered. If Jesus asked, would you start with the questions?

Or money? What do I want? Well, I don't need to be a billionaire, I'm not trying to be greedy, but if I just had enough to, you know, get everything all caught-up, and maybe enough to give some to the kids to help them, and maybe retirement. You know, just enough. Would you maybe ask for that?

Or maybe just a simple little miracle to cure that illness, or heal that wound, or mend that broken relationship, or... just a little miracle, nothing like parting an ocean, I'm not trying to be selfish. Just give me this one, little, miracle?

"What do you want?" Jesus asked the two guys with John. They didn't seem to hesitate. They asked, "Where are you staying?" In other words, "Can we hang with you for a while?" Wow! I have to be honest with you and say that I'm a bit embarrassed to say that one didn't even cross my mind. It wasn't even on my list. Can we just spend some time with you, get to know you, find out what you're really like? Jesus said, "Sure. Come on. Let's go." John's disciples went with Jesus and spent the day with him.

That bit about "the man who comes after me and would end up going past me because he had already here before me" doesn't seem all that important to me at this point. Not compared to, "What do you want?"

Then, I come to the line where John wrote, "It was about four in the afternoon." What in the heck is significant about four in the afternoon? Why did John include that? Was this another of those Greek things that John knew about that I don't? Then I remember. One of the key principles of the first-century community was that it was extremely important to treat visitors and guests as you would want to be treated by them. If it was mealtime, invite them to eat. If it was getting late and they were away from home, invite them to stay the night. That was just how things were done - most of the time. Sometimes, those members of the community who were in positions of authority and power did not believe it was proper to offer that openness to people of less station. They might suggest a few places where a meal or a bed might be found, but surely they couldn't be expected to bring them into their own home. Four o'clock was the beginning of the evening time, and apparently, they had traveled far enough from where they first met Jesus to make that an issue. As the two men were standing in the courtyard debating about where to find a meal and room, Jesus walked over and said, "You two better get washed up for dinner. I hope you like lamb." After dinner, they were given a bedroll.

At this point, I find it hard to even remember that line about someone coming before me and passing me because he was... whatever. Now my mind is reeling as I ask myself how I might have dealt with the two visitors. I would like to believe I would have thrown some extra chicken on the grill, and pulled out the futon in the guest room. I would like to believe that. But I can't be certain. There are a lot of "it depends" involved. What did the two guys look like? Did they look trustworthy? Were they clean? As I said, I would like to believe... but I'm not going to worry too much about that right now because the toughest line of all is coming next.

John then told us that one of the two men that spent the day with Jesus was named Andrew. The day after the visit, when they returned home, John said that the first thing Andrew did was hunt down his brother, Simon, and tell him, "We have found the Christ!"

And here, I'm pretty much at my limit. These two guys spent part of one day following Jesus around and ended up drawing the conclusion that he was the one, true, Son of God. There is now only one thought running through my mind. Just one. I wonder what conclusion two people would come to if they spent the day following me around? I mean, I can do a pretty good imitation of a disciple when I put my mind to it; when I keep focused and think about what I am doing and saying. But an entire day? What would the two guys think about me?

I think I'm going to stop here. I'm still not sure I understand what John was saying with that line back at the beginning. But I think I clearly understand what he was saying there at the end. Those who follow me through my day, co-workers, friends, and family — when the day comes to a close, what do they conclude about me?

What do they conclude about me?

Amen.

# The Big Move!

Just so you know, we are going to use our imaginations today. We're not going to just kind of play around and make things up, but we are going to use our imaginations to see if we find some new meaning in a passage we have probably read or heard many times before. We're going to try and remember what was going on back in the first century when this story actually took place and see if that might give us any new thoughts about why John wrote this down.

John was writing about what happened when John the Baptist was finally arrested and put in prison, and Jesus moved to Galilee where he started collecting his disciples. It sounds so simple and clean as John told it; pretty calm and straightforward. Jesus heard that John was in prison. He took that as the sign that it was time for him to begin his ministry, so he moved to Galilee and started gathering his disciples. It makes sense. But let's see if we can get an idea of what it might have been like when it happened, through the eyes of those living it.

We're going to begin in Nazareth, only fifteen or twenty miles from the Sea of Galilee, but an entire world apart culturally. Nazareth was a small town in traditional Jewish territory, on a hill overlooking a valley filled with stories told in the Old Testament. It was far enough from Jerusalem that the Romans didn't pay them that much attention. The people were small town, hard-working, synagogue-going families. And for Jesus, this was home.

Galilee was different. The Roman client, king Herod Antipas built a city near the hot springs on the edge of the sea and named it after the Roman Emperor, Tiberius. He made it the capital of his realm, and it became such an important city that for a while the Sea of Galilee was known as the Sea of Tiberius. It was a Roman city, filled with all things Roman, and considered ritually unclean to the Jews. But Tiberius attracted travelers from all around the world, and many of them stayed and settled in other towns in the area. As close as it was to Nazareth, they were not the same. The idea that a nice Jewish boy from Nazareth would pack up and move to Galilee would have raised some eyebrows. Jesus was from Nazareth, but he had traveled around and even made several trips down south to Jerusalem. We know some of the stories of how, even as a child, he spent time arguing with the religious leaders at the temple. He traveled around the Jordan River, including the day he met John there and was baptized. But each time, he ended up returning home to Nazareth. Nazareth was home. It was safe. Whatever he was becoming in the rest of the land, and whatever God was turning him into, back in Nazareth he was still seen as Joseph and Mary's boy, smart as a whip, but learning his father's trade and most likely going to find a nice girl and end up settling down in a nice little house in town.

My guess is that it was not all quite that simple. My guess is that there were some in Nazareth who had questions. In my mind, some of the folks in Nazareth that were Jesus' age used to make comments about him out wandering around the countryside, showing off, trying to be more than he was; a simple small town boy from the country. I can imagine the old men sitting at that round table at the back of the coffee shop every morning, talking about how shameful it was for that boy to be out running all over the place, leaving his aging father to take care of the shop all by himself. I even wonder if they were the first ones to talk about that prodigal son thing Jesus would mention a couple of years later? And when Mary walked down the street or brought her casserole to the synagogue potlucks, the other women put on their sad faces and said, "Poor Mary. How are you getting along dear?" Nazareth was a small town, and there would have been expectations of sons born there.

We actually don't know much at all about what Jesus did between his birth and his baptism. There are lots of other writings and stories, but most of them are just someone using their imaginations like we are doing now. We don't know what it was that caused Jesus to decide when it was time to get baptized if he knew it was the beginning of what was to come, or if he just went there because he was curious like all the others. All we know is that one day after that, someone showed up in Nazareth with the news that John had been arrested and was in a prison out in the wilderness. And for some reason, Jesus made a decision.

John made it sound so simple. When Jesus heard that John had been put in prison, he withdrew to Galilee. It sounds like Jesus heard the news, put his hammer over on the workbench, picked up his jacket, and walked out the door with a determined look on his face. But I wonder.

First, why was he going? Why Galilee? Why now? What did John mean that he "withdrew"? Moving from a tiny and safe country town to a place filled with Romans and other unclean things doesn't sound all that much like withdrawing to me. It sounds more like that "out of the frying pan into the fire" thing to me. And, could he just walk away and leave everything like that? Even if he understood who he was and what he needed to do, could he just leave home and family so easily? John's simple little story creates so many questions in my mind.

Nazareth was a very small town, maybe two to three hundred people or so. Nobody just slipped away. The culture would not have allowed it. There would have been some type of farewell thing, at least another potluck in the basement of the synagogue, maybe a few speeches, probably with those old men sitting at a table in the back of the room shaking their heads, and the old women standing closely around Mary to give her strength, "Poor Mary." At a minimum, a few folks would have dropped by the house to offer their best wishes and remind Jesus of the various laws he was going to have to be careful to remember if he was really going to go hang out with Romans and other non-Jewish people. As Jesus left, Dad would have been out on the sidewalk just to offer a few final words and to watch his son walk down the street, out of sight around the corner. After that, in my mind,

Joseph went back out to his shop and just spent some time looking around, remembering. Mary and Joseph would have spent a very quiet night that night. Nothing sounded good for dinner, nothing good to watch on TV, and sleep would not have come easily to either of them. No, in my mind it would not have just been a simple leaving. Even if Jesus and everyone else knew exactly who he was and what he had to do, for the people of Nazareth he was still Joseph and Mary's boy. And he was leaving.

Why did he go to Galilee, and what was he withdrawing from?

Although Nazareth was a long way from Jerusalem, what happened at Jesus' baptism would have been big news at the temple. Remember that Pharisees and Sadducees had been there when it happened and would have made a bee-line trip back to report what they had seen and heard. And while the Jews of Nazareth would have cut Jesus some slack because he was a local boy, those from outside of town would not have been so understanding. This Jesus of Nazareth was beginning to stir things up. First, we had this John guy running around claiming to wash people's sins away. That was creating enough trouble. People were beginning to question the old laws. Some were even beginning to challenge the authority of some of those Pharisees and Sadducees, which is something that could simply not be tolerated. Now it appeared that this small town country boy was trying to increase the pressure.

As big as John was getting, he wasn't really that much of a threat. He did a good job of dressing and playing the part of a prophet, but so had all the others before him, and they never lasted, so he won't either. But this Jesus from

Nazareth didn't dress funny, and he didn't run around ranting and raving. He seemed to have an uncanny understanding of the old books, and of the law. He was different and that got the attention of those very powerful people. My hunch is that they had sent people to Nazareth to check this guy out. Nazareth was small enough that these visitors would not have gone unnoticed, and when they walked into the café in the morning the entire room went silent. Jesus would have known about them, and he would have understood. Nazareth was still home, but it was no longer safe. And it would get worse.

My guess is that Jesus knew the showdown with the temple was coming, but he also knew that he was not ready for it yet. Not if he wanted to make sure his message would live long after he was finished. That was going to take followers. Galilee not only had lots of potential followers, but it was also a place the religious leaders from Jerusalem did not like to go. Galilee would be the perfect place to avoid too early of a confrontation, and a place to find his disciples. He withdrew to Galilee.

That gives me one other thought before we stop.

We've only been imagining some things here, but I wonder if it might remind us of something that Jesus seemed to understand that we sometimes forget. When you are going to do battle with evil, you need to prepare. Part of that preparation is to see that you do not enter into that battle alone. If that was important enough for Jesus to remember, I'm thinking it's worth our remembering as well.

We may never feel called to confront something with the power of the Pharisees, Sadducees, and priests of Jerusalem, but we may be called to stand against misguided leaders of our world today. We may be called to do battle with an uncontrolled temper or an addiction, or to stand up in support of someone being abused, being left in the cold without food or protection, or without the opportunity to be the child that God created them to become. Whatever the battle, our winning is more assured if we do not take it on by ourselves but find others who will stand beside us, and who will continue the battle if and when we have done all we can do.

This may just be my mind working here, but I can imagine what it would be like if this was how we saw ourselves as the church that Jesus left behind. I can imagine what that church would be like if it never allowed someone to fight their battles alone. If, instead of standing on the edge offering words prayers of support, collecting occasional donations of money, and posting lots of neat messages and pictures on social networks, if that church stepped right out there and stood next to the person doing battle and said, "We are here with you. We will fight alongside you. This is now our fight too. Together, we will win this battle."

It may just be my imagination, but wow, can you imagine seeing that kind of church?

Can you imagine being that kind of church?

Just imagine.

Amen.

Epiphany 4

Matthew 5:1-12

# The Challenge Of Simplicity

The crowds had grown. Jesus had been in Galilee for a while now, speaking, healing, and calling his disciples to follow him. The leaders from Jerusalem certainly had their spies keeping an eye on him, but with the crowds he was gathering, all they could do right now was watch and listen. Wherever Jesus went, there were always a few Pharisees and Sadducees in the crowd looking for things he might do or say they could use against him when they did finally get the chance. His disciples occasionally reminded him of the risk and seemed confused when he didn't seem to care. It was almost like he was intentionally trying to make them angry, like today.

Today, Jesus is walking along the road just a mile or so west of Capernaum where he was living now. Along with his disciples, there was a large group of people following him, and more coming down the roads from all directions. Jesus looked around for a spot open enough to hold everyone and found a place to sit down. Jesus watched as the crowd gathered around him: fishermen, farmers, orchard keepers, shopkeepers, mothers, children, and others. Pharisees and Sadducees from Jerusalem; they were there too.

Jesus began speaking. Unfortunately, many of us have never heard what he said that day. Matthew wrote about it, and so did Luke. We've read what they wrote and have even given part of his message that day a title of its own. We call that part the Beatitudes. You've probably heard several sermons and Sunday school lessons about the Beatitudes. We hear and talk a lot "about" the Beatitudes, but I wonder if many of us have actually heard what Jesus said?

Most of the time we get distracted and end up talking about or debating other things. For example, Matthew told us that Jesus and the group were on a mountain when he spoke these words. Luke said they were on a flat plain somewhere. And someone usually points out that there really weren't any mountains around that area. So we debate. Where were they? Was Matthew correct or was Luke? Can we really say that one of the gospel writers was wrong? We get distracted.

Then someone points out that Matthew writes about the eight Beatitudes that Jesus mentioned, while Luke only has four in his version. What do we do with that? We find some historians who argue that Jesus did not speak the Beatitudes on a mountain or on a plain, but they were part of what Jesus said that day he sat on the boat and spoke to the crowds gathered on the shore.

While these things make great subjects for seminary theology classes, it seems to me that most of the time they are just distractions. We debate back and forth about these questions and end up just glancing at what Jesus was actually saying that day. I really don't think it matters where he said it: mountain, plain, boat, on the dock at

Josiah's Bait and Tackle Shop; it doesn't change what he said. For just a few minutes, I'd like to see if we can tune out some of the distractions and hear the Beatitudes.

But before we begin, I need to warn you that this is going to be difficult at times — not difficult to understand what Jesus was saying; that's not difficult at all. Jesus had the take on things that other people made complex, and he was good at explaining them in ways that made them clear enough for the uneducated crowd around him to understand. That is what makes this difficult. Not understanding what Jesus was saying, but trying to figure out what we're going to do after we do actually understand. Sometimes it is going to be difficult, and that's why we spend so much time focusing on the distractions rather than what he said.

Distraction is a powerful thing. Politicians use it to keep us from paying attention to more important things. Armies use it to cause their enemy to look in one direction while they build to attack from another. Marketers use distraction to keep us from paying attention to the reasons we might not want to buy their product or philosophy, or from the obvious false promises they are making. Distractions keep us from having to deal with the hard questions. If the preacher can preach a sermon about whether Jesus was on a mountain or a plain, we don't have to worry about the sermon saying something that might really put us in a tough spot.

So just a warning: this may become difficult at times.

Jesus sat down, which is what a teacher did when they were going to say something really important. The crowd grew quiet and everyone leaned forward to catch every word. Then he began.

*Blessed are the poor in spirit, for theirs is the kingdom of heaven.*

This won't take long. Everyone there got it much quicker than we do. They knew poor in spirit. When Jesus said it, most of the crowd turned and glanced at the little group of Pharisees and Sadducees. Those guys defined rich in spirit. Poor in spirit wasn't just talking about money, it was about a spirit that does not become proud. The Pharisees and Sadducees stood out from the crowd. Their fancy robes with colors, stoles, and big hats with jewels and do-dads on them. They were proud of their faith because they knew that their faith was the right faith, and that meant they were right. Their spirits were anything but poor. They caught what Jesus was saying, as well as the looks from the crowd and they made notes about it.

In this comment and the others that followed, Jesus was making a clear point. He was giving the crowd a list. He was telling them the eight things you need to do if you want to follow him. Each one of the eight things was simple. And together, they spoke a very simple message. If you want to follow me, you do things differently. Different from the old ways. Different from those guys over there with the fancy robes and hats. If you want to follow Jesus, you have to be different. First of all, if you are following Jesus, don't ever get the idea that it is something to boast or show-off about.

Give me a minute here; I need to refocus. I always get a bit distracted by this one. I have to be honest and admit that sometimes, when I remember this one, I look around at what we sometimes do and I wonder. I look at our buildings, our sanctuaries, the things that might be seen as our robes and fancy hats, and I have to pause. I remind myself that if we are using these things to communicate Jesus' message in the best way for people to hear today we're probably okay. But if we ever begin to feel proud of these things, or that we deserve these things, I think we may be in a bit of trouble. Others may boast; we have to be different than that. Can you see the look on the faces of the Pharisees yet?

*Blessed are those who mourn.*

Everyone mourns at some point, even Pharisees and Sadducees. We mourn at the loss of someone we care for, or for some harm that comes to someone we care for. But Jesus wasn't talking just about those folks. Blessed are those who look at the world in the condition it is in now, and they mourn. They don't just empathize enough to send a nice card or flowers, but their heard aches at how some other people are being treated; even people they do not know and will never meet. They mourn. They are blessed.

*Blessed are the meek.*

This is a tough one for our culture. We respond by insisting that businesses and nations are not created through meekness but through determination and strength. We end up distracted, arguing about whether or not Jesus was pro-business. Or, debating about whether or not the amount of wealth and property controlled by the church today disqualifies them from being "meek." But Jesus isn't talking about money and property here, and he is not saying that if you want to follow him you need to become a wimp. He is talking about humility. You may be wealthy or poor, you may have great power or very little. Whatever you are, be humble. Never consider yourself to be of more value than someone else, regardless of any circumstances. And having humility means, no matter what, never seeking vengeance. The Pharisees wrote the book on vengeance. Jesus was saying to be different than the Pharisees and Sadducees. They made a note of that one too.

In my imagination, it was at this point that Jesus noticed the movement in the crowd. Many of them had come a long way and started out really early this morning to get here. They were quite a distance from a town, and some of the group was clearly getting hungry and thirsty. In my mind, one of the Pharisees opened a bag one of his aides had picked up at the Tiberius coffee house and pulled out a nice pineapple scone he started to munch on while he sipped his caramel cappuccino with extra foam. Jesus looked at them and said:

*Blessed are those who hunger and thirst after righteousness.*

Righteousness isn't the same thing as being right, however right the Pharisees might be in enforcing the old laws, they the exact opposite of righteous. Righteousness means justice. Jesus was saying that you can create as many laws as you want, but if they are not founded in justice for everyone, you can never be considered to be righteous. The Pharisees were the perfect example of what it meant to be people of faith. I'm betting Jesus was looking right at them as he told the group that if they wanted to follow him, they needed to be the exact opposite. The Pharisee almost choked on his scone.

*Blessed are the merciful.*

I think Jesus was asking that when you look around you at other people, do you see them through your own eyes, or do you try to see them through their eyes and try to understand who they are and why they are where they are? Do you hold people to a standard that fits your view of the world and how you were raised, or do you try to understand why they might appear to have a different standard? When you absolutely disagree with someone's views or actions, do you write them off or go on the attack, do you try to understand that person is a just a human being with a different opinion than your own? When someone clearly makes a mistake, do you define them by that mistake or try to understand what led to it happening and try to understand there is more to that person than that one mistake? Pharisees lived in a simple world. You either agreed with them and followed the laws and were right or you broke the laws and were wrong. Jesus said you have to be different.

*Blessed are the pure in heart.*

Jesus knew that no one in that crowd was pure. But he knew that even those who made mistakes could have the very best of intentions; they could be pure in heart. We all make honest mistakes. But some, once again giving a nod to the Pharisees and Sadducees, some are never quite what they present themselves to be. They approach you as a friend and watch for ways to attack you. They speak of justice and love and then pounce on you when you slip-up. They talk about God's love, and then angrily attack you when you disagree with their views. Some people are always planning and plotting. Everything they do is a step to position themselves for some next step on their list. They may truly care about someone or something, but there are reasons. They may have hearts of compassion, but that compassion is there to help them achieve something else. This is like the loyal and devout old gentleman who hasn't missed a Sunday service in 47 years, who gives more than his tithe, and who offers his smile and prayers freely and openly. But it is not pure. He expects something in return. It might be to have a louder voice in the decision-making at the church, or maybe it's just that he believes his actions are securing him that ticket through those pearly gates when that day comes. He is not offering his heart purely, but in the way the Pharisee offers theirs. "I love you… and therefore…." Jesus said you have to be different.

*Blessed are the peacemakers.*

Ah, finally one we can deal with. We realize that when we talk about peace, we might be talking about peace between countries, or peace between people in town, or even just peace in our families. But regardless, we are all in support of peace. We try to get along with people. We go out of our way to even be polite to those folks we had the argument with years ago. We don't hang out together, but if we happen to bump into each other at church or something we are polite. We support peace. But Jesus did not say, "Blessed are those who support peace." He said peacemakers. Blessed are those who do the things that are required to do to create peace, to bring peace where there is now no peace. Blessed are those who make peace happen.

But, but, but... can you hear the distractions: the interpretations of that simple statement? Hey, I'm just here where I live. I don't have the power to make countries quit fighting. I'll vote for the person I think might do that, but what else can I do? My hunch is that there are still a few opportunities for peacemaking within our reach such as broken relationships. Remember, Jesus didn't say that we're blessed if we do our best to be polite, or if we say that we'll stop calling that other person names, or that we'll accept their apology if and when they offer it. Jesus said blessed are those who do make peace happen. Blessed are those who don't just hope for it or wait for someone to offer it, but those who get up in the morning and spend their day to make peace happen.

I have always liked the passage in some of the rituals for the Lords' Supper near the beginning that says something like, "if you have any broken relationships or have anyone with whom you are at odds, go and make it right and then come forward to Christ's table." I've read it hundreds of times, but I've always wondered what would happen if anyone really listened to it? I wonder how many would actually just get up out of their pew and walk up to that altar like they always do. I wonder if I would even stay there to see, or if I would be honest and hop in my car to go find those folks I needed to patch things up with before I came back to hand out the little cups and crackers?

Instead, I stay distracted. I focus on remembering the other things I need to do in the ritual, making sure we keep the lines moving and the spills cleaned up because distractions are easier than actually listening to what Jesus expects us to do.

By this point, the Pharisees and Sadducees had looks on their faces that were scaring the crowd. At first, they all looked the Pharisees and Sadducees and smiled when

Jesus said something, but then they were afraid to look. One of the Pharisees might remember their face later. That would not be good. I think Jesus noticed that.

*Blessed are those who are persecuted for righteousness' sake, for theirs is the kingdom of heaven.*

Jesus knew what the crowd was thinking. If they actually did the things he was telling them to do, if they were really as different as he said they needed to be, they were going to end up in a heap of trouble. Even way up there in Galilee, if you went against the temple leaders long enough they would find out and come and get you. You could get arrested. You could lose your home or business. For crying out loud, you could even end up being crucified. If Jesus had a modern day public relations person among his disciples, he probably would have suggested that Jesus speak this last one really, really fast, like those things at the end of a drug commercial on television. Yes, they could be persecuted, and we really ought to warn them, but let's tell them really quickly so it doesn't spoil the effect of everything else you've talked about. The PR guy would have recommended using distraction but Jesus kept it simple and short. That's why this whole thing is so darned difficult.

Being a follower of Jesus of Nazareth is not a difficult thing to understand. We talk and write a lot about it, and we create lots of extra activities and traditions that we say are a part of being a follower, or at least things that we think followers ought to be doing too. But as Jesus presented it that day, wherever the heck it was, it was not complicated at all.

Following Jesus might be the most difficult thing we've ever tried to do, but don't let anyone tell you it's complicated.

Amen.

Epiphany 5

Matthew 5:13-20

# Righteous, Dude!

The first thing I need to say is to point out that the story today picks up right where we left off last time. Jesus was sitting somewhere near the Sea of Galilee teaching a large crowd of people who had come to hear him. Along with the usual people who lived and worked in the villages and towns around the sea, there was a group of Pharisees and Sadducees who had been sent up from Jerusalem to check this Jesus out and determine if he was going to become a problem. So far, they had taken a lot of notes. Jesus started off with those lines we call the Beatitudes, eight things that Jesus said people needed to do if they were going to be one of his followers. In short, they all simply said that if you want to follow Jesus and be true to God, you needed to do everything exactly opposite of what the Pharisees and Sadducees did. Yeah, I think they were beginning to believe he might be becoming a problem.

He had just finished warning everyone that if they did decide to follow him, they would most likely be persecuted. I'll just say that I think he nodded his head toward the Pharisees and Sadducees when he said: "persecuted." It just seems to fit, especially as we hear what he had to say next.

Jesus took this opportunity to tell a couple of short little stories about things everyone there would be familiar with so they would get the point. He began by talking about salt. It helps things make sense if we remember that these folks would have all had salt in their homes, just like most of us do. But they didn't have that little round container with the umbrella on it sitting in their cupboard. The Pharisees probably had some kind of fancy salt dispenser in their homes, most likely something in silver or gold with a few jewels on it for good measure. But the rest of the crowd would have just had their salt-rock to deal with. It was the cheapest way to purchase salt. You simply went to the salt vendor and bought one of the rocks they had collected from the salt mine, or from the shores of the Great Sea about thirty miles away to the west. It was just as it sounds. It was a rock that was coated in layers of salt that was left after the seawater evaporated. When someone wanted salt, they picked up the grapefruit-sized rock from the middle of the table and scraped off as much salt as they wanted. It worked just fine. But, after a while, someone would scrape off the last layer of salt, and all you then had left was a rock. So when Jesus said something about what happens when salt loses its saltiness, people in the crowd smiled and looked at each other, thinking of all the times that had happened in their homes.

Jesus asked them what value the rock had when all the salt was gone. They would have laughed because it was an obvious answer. Unless you were a collector of old rocks, when salt lost its saltiness it was of no use whatsoever. I think the Pharisees were left shaking their heads. At least he had finally stopped going after them.

But then Jesus said, "You are the salt of the earth." In other words, here it comes again. Your purpose as one of my followers is to change the taste of things in this world. That is your role. If you choose to not follow the eight things we just talked about a few minutes ago, you are of no more value to God than that rock you threw out the window the last time the salt was gone. Salt changes things. You are the salt of the world. He was clearly not finished with those Pharisees and Sadducees standing in the group.

To understand what came next it will help to understand more about where we believe they were meeting that day. The traditional spot of the meeting was about a mile or so west of the town of Capernaum, and about a half mile away from the sea itself. The land sloped gently up to where Jesus was sitting, and a few miles further north the land swept up to a higher range of hills. Up there on the top of those hills is a highway. It runs from over in what used to be Babylonia, across the northern part of Israel, then all the way down to Egypt. It is a busy route for business and trading and was filled with travelers from nations from all over the world. And along the highway were towns larger than those down here around the Sea of Galilee. At night, if you looked to the north, you could see the lights of those grand cities glowing in the darkness.

They all knew the story about what happened many years ago when Babylonia and Egypt were fighting. Just like today's travelers, as the enemy armies moved across the land to fight each other, they traveled that same highway. And, as often happens, as the armies traveled through towns that were not their own, they did their share of sacking and pillaging, leaving their trail of destruction as they moved. During one of those periods, one of those towns on the hill tried to protect itself from the traveling armies which frequently traveled by night when it was cooler. When word arrived that an army was drawing near, everyone in that town turned out their lights at night, hoping the armies would pass right by without even noticing them. I'm not sure how well it worked, but everyone knew the story.

When Jesus said, "a town built on a hill cannot be hidden" everyone in the group would have automatically turned and looked to the north and understood what he was saying. He said that if they were worried about persecution they could certainly hide what they were doing, but that's not what his true followers would do. The followers of Jesus would not light their lamp and then hide it under a bowl to avoid being seen by their enemies. They would put light enough lamps to lighten the entire house and be visible enough that everyone around them would see what they were doing and be inspired by it. Yes, it might bring the enemy. But, our faith is larger than they were.

I think the crowd would have fully understood but I don't think they wore the same smiles they had with the thing about the salt. I think there were glances at the Pharisees and Sadducees again. And perhaps the Pharisees were smiling. They had been concerned while he made the comments about how bad he thought the Pharisees and Sadducees were. But that wasn't something they could do anything about. This was Roman territory, and Rome was not all that interested in how anyone treated Pharisees and Sadducees. He was encouraging these people to stand up and be noticed. This sounded a lot like he was inciting a rebellion. This was something that could get Rome's attention. I'm thinking Jesus may have seen their smiles, and he decided to drive his message home once and for all. I think he turned his words directly to the Pharisees.

He said, "Do not think that I have come to abolish the law or the prophets; I have not come to abolish them but to fulfill them." The Pharisees looked up. Everything Jesus had said so far was an attack on the practices of the temple in Jerusalem, which was clearly an attack on the laws of Moses themselves. But now? If he wasn't out to abolish the laws, what was he trying to accomplish? If he came out in support of the laws of Moses that would make it far more difficult for them to convince Jerusalem to see him as a threat. Maybe they had scared him enough he was backpedaling a bit.

The crowd was silent. Wait a minute. I thought he had been talking about helping free us from the sometimes cruel control of the legal wizards from Jerusalem, and here he is saying he is here to fulfill those laws? The Pharisees and Sadducees stood with their mouths open. Did Jesus just say what it sounded like he said?

Jesus kept going. He went on to say that the laws of Moses will stay around until heaven and earth themselves disappear, and until that happens, not one punctuation mark in those laws is going to be changed.

Was that a cheer I just heard from the Pharisee and Sadducee crowd?

He said that any person who did anything to change or ignore any of the laws, even the smallest of them, would end up becoming the least important person in the kingdom of heaven... the front seats in heaven were reserved for those who practiced the laws as they were meant to be practiced.

The crowd was completely confused; except for the folks in the fancy robes and hats. In my mind, a few folks had gotten up and started walking to the back of the crowd. They had had enough. I think that might have happened, because I know if I had been there I would be one of them. "After all of the stuff he said earlier; the things he said that gave us some hope. And now he turns out to sound just like all the rest of those false prophets who talk loud and strong for a while and then chicken out. I am just tired of these people who come up with their promises, and then just leave me hanging when the pressure is on. I'm going home." Yeah, I think that might have been me.

The Pharisees and Sadducees were ripping up their notes and making plans to start the journey back to Jerusalem. Just like those who had come before, this Jesus started out strong but ended up toeing the line. There would be no need to bother the Romans about this one.

However, just as those leaving were getting out of earshot, they heard Jesus say, "For I tell you that unless your righteousness surpasses that of the Pharisees and the teachers of the law, you will certainly not enter the kingdom of heaven."

The folks leaving stopped walking. Cheers broke out around the crowd, no one cared anymore about being seen by the Pharisees and Sadducees. Everyone there believed what Jesus just said. They had believed it for a long time but no one had ever had the courage to say it out loud. And no one had ever even thought of saying it with Pharisees and Sadducees standing right in front of them. Now they understood that this Jesus from Nazareth was something different from the others. They may not have yet been convinced he was the actual Son of God, but they were absolutely certain he was someone they wanted to listen to.

The Pharisees and Sadducees were the experts on the laws of Moses. They memorized them. They spent every day of their lives interpreting and enforcing the laws of Moses. But they did not live their lives according to the laws of Moses. They recognized the words of those laws, but not the meaning. Outwardly, they were holy, law-abiding, and God-fearing leaders of the Jewish nation. But too often beneath the robes, they were corrupt, self-serving thieves, using God as an excuse for doing anything they wanted to do. Everyone knew it, but no one had ever said it.

The Pharisees and Sadducees just stared at him. Every eye in the crowd was locked on them. But there was nothing they could do. Not here. Not now. After a few minutes, I think the Pharisees probably turned and left the group now, and started the trip back home. They couldn't do anything about it right now, but they had come to a decision. This Jesus of Nazareth had to go.

Salt changes things. Lights change things. You are the salt of the earth and you are the light of the world. Let your light so shine before people that they may see what you are doing and will give glory to God.

In short, you are to be different.

Amen.

Epiphany 6

Matthew 5:21-37

# Brace Yourself!

Before we look at today's scripture, let's take a moment to remember where we were and what was going on. After John the Baptist was arrested, Jesus moved from Nazareth to Galilee where he could do what he needed to do to prepare for his ministry. Galilee was more Roman than Jewish, so the Pharisees and Sadducees in Jerusalem would have less ability to stop him before he was ready. He traveled the area preaching, teaching, and finding those who would become his disciples. One day as they were walking along the northern shore of the sea a large group of people started to gather around them. Jesus found a spot big enough to hold them all and sat down to teach them. Looking around the crowd, he saw fishermen, farmers, orchard-keepers, mothers, and children, all eager to hear what he had to say. Over to one side, he saw the little group of those Pharisees and Sadducees dressed in their fine robes and hats, wearing their stoles and jewelry. They didn't have enough authority to arrest him up there, but if they could catch him saying things against the temple they might be able to get him the next time he came down to Jerusalem. Jesus saw them and he knew what they were thinking. Everyone knew what they were thinking.

The Pharisees and Sadducees were powerful. They were the country's religious leaders. They knew the laws of Moses better than anyone and spent their time making sure that everyone followed those laws and did what they were supposed to do. They were powerful men. They were held up as the example of what it meant to be holy; to be one of God's children. In reality, many of them were corrupt and cruel, using their positions to fill their own pockets and protect their positions. Everyone here in the group today knew that, but no one dared say it. Pharisees and Sadducees were just too powerful.

Jesus talked to the group in plain and simple language. Pharisees and Sadducees talked in circles, using fancy words from a language no one even spoke anymore — no one except Pharisees and Sadducees. That's how they kept everyone confused. That's how they kept their control. But Jesus made it very easy for them to understand what he had to say today. Instead of trying to figure out what he was saying, they ended up having to figure out what they were going to do about what he said. That was harder. If we don't really understand something we can just kind of ignore it and say, "I wasn't really sure what you meant." But if something is very clear and we choose not to do it, the excuses can be more difficult to find.

Jesus spoke to them about the things you needed to do if you wanted to follow him. He told them that if they wanted to be a part of the kingdom of God, they needed to be different. They needed to be like salt that changes everything it touches. They needed to be like light that removes darkness from the world. Then he told them what it meant to be different. He said that if you want to

116

be a part of the kingdom of God, you needed to be more righteous than the Pharisees and Sadducees. To serve God, you had to be different than them.

He had just made that simple and clear statement as we read today's passage from Matthew. Every person in the crowd understood what he meant. The guys in the fancy robes and hats were furious. The rest of the crowd was smiling, maybe even cheering, to finally find someone with the courage to call a snake a snake. They knew the Pharisees and Sadducees were not righteous. They were golden on the outside and nothing but mud on the inside. It really shouldn't be that difficult to be more righteous than those guys.

Then Jesus made it tougher. In my mind, he saw their smiles and realized they didn't really understand just what he was meant by being righteous. So I think he said: "Let me give you an example."

"You have heard that it was said to the people long ago, 'You shall not murder, and anyone who murders will be subject to judgment.'"

Everyone nodded. They had learned that concept as children. They all agreed with that one.

"But I tell you that anyone who is angry with a brother or sister will be subject to judgment."

Can you see their faces? "What did he say?" While the odds are that none of the folks there would ever commit murder, most everyone there had brothers and sisters, and like most families that meant arguments. Was he really serious?

Jesus kept going and said that anyone who calls his brother or sister a fool is in danger of the fires of hell. What? Wait a minute.

He wasn't finished.

"If you are offering your gift at the altar and there remember that your brother or sister has something against you, leave your gift there in front of the altar. First go and be reconciled to them; then come and offer your gift."

He kept going.

"And if you are taking someone to court over some issue, go to them quickly and get it settled. If you go before a judge, you are the one who will end up paying for it."

In my mind, a couple of business owners in the group immediately thought about the charges they had just filed against the people who owed them money. And the two guys who were in the middle of the legal battle over that property line in the backyard gave each other a quick glance. Is he serious? I mean, murder is one thing, but really?

Jesus' words were simple. Simple enough to understand. That's what makes them so difficult.

He then looked around and said:

"You have heard that it was said, 'You shall not commit adultery.'"

They nodded. At least we're back to something we can deal with.

"But I tell you that anyone who has ever looked at someone and had lustful thoughts has already committed adultery in their heart."

In my mind, two guys give a nervous glance at each other thinking about what they had said as they walked here this morning and passed those girls waiting at the well. And I think someone in the crowd wanted to ask, "Just how lustful of a thought does it have to be?" He wanted to spend some time to find the loopholes in this new interpretation of the law. There were always loopholes weren't there? But Jesus had already moved on.

"It has been said, 'Anyone who divorces his wife must give her a certificate of divorce.'"

It would have been difficult to find a family in the crowd that hadn't dealt with this one in one way or another. The old law said that a man could divorce his wife anytime he found something disgraceful about her. In the beginning, that probably meant that she had committed adultery or something like that. But over the years the loopholes were created. A wife doing something disgraceful might mean she had put too much of that salt in the gravy, or she had grown too old to be as good to look at as the younger woman down the road.

According to the old law, to divorce his wife all the man had to do was to hand his wife a piece of paper with the words, "I Josiah, divorce you Elizabeth", and it was done. Over time, the wives became smarter and did things like standing on a table so the husband could not reach her with the piece of paper. The law was then amended to say that all the husband had to do was throw the piece of paper at the woman's feet. Then the guy came home with the paper to find his wife standing on the roof. No matter how hard he tried, he couldn't get the paper high enough in the air. So the law was amended so he just had to read the words to her in the presence of two witnesses. Wives could be creative, so the laws were constantly being revised. It was a mess.

Jesus looked at them and said:

"It has been said, 'Anyone who divorces his wife must give her a certificate of divorce.'"

They listened.

"But I tell you that anyone who divorces his wife, except for sexual immorality, makes her the victim of adultery, and anyone who marries a divorced woman commits adultery."

Okay...we need to pause here a minute. Was Jesus actually saying that the only grounds for a divorce are sexual infidelity? What about abandonment? What about addiction? What about abuse? What about physical cruelty, or mental cruelty? Was Jesus really saying the man or woman experiencing any of those things just have to stay put and endure it?

We all know that many who say, "Yes, that is exactly what Jesus is saying." This passage from Matthew was the proof they needed. But for right now, I'm going to ask that we wait a few minutes before we do more with this one. We're not going to ignore it, and I'm not just going to accept it without trying to understand if that is indeed what Jesus is saying to us. But I think it might help if we let Jesus finish the rest of what he had to say and then come back to look at this one again.

The crowd was as uneasy as we may be now. Jesus had suddenly sounded about as harsh as those men in the robes and fancy hats. I think he knew that, and I think that's why he went on to say:

"Again, you have heard that it was said to the people long ago, 'Do not break your oath, but fulfill to the Lord the vows you have made."

There were a lot of laws about making oaths or promises. You could make an oath by swearing on heaven, or on Jerusalem, or on your own head. There were ways you could assure someone you would not break the promise you were making to them. There were many, many laws describing the specific steps you needed to take to swear an oath. There were many laws about how to make a promise and each of those laws had enough loopholes to make it simple to break any oath one might make, including the oath of marriage. Remember that guy trying to throw that piece of paper up to his roof? At some point, he had followed the law to make an oath to his wife and yet he was using the loopholes to break that promise.

Jesus then said:

"All you need to say is simply 'Yes' or 'No'; anything beyond this comes from the evil one."

Making a promise is not about following laws. A promise is a simple "Yes", or a simple "No." It is not a list of laws that come with loopholes. A promise is not something we make based on heaven, or Jerusalem, or anything else. A promise is something that we make ourselves, something that we alone are responsible for. If that promise is broken, I am the one who chose to break it. Me…it is that simple.

Let's go back now and look at what Jesus said a few minutes ago about divorce. I know what I am going to say may not sit well with everyone here. And I cannot guarantee that what I am going to say is absolutely what

Jesus meant that day. But as I watch what Jesus said and did after that day on the hillside, I believe it fits with the rest of his message.

A marriage is an oath made by two people. A marriage is a third thing that is created when two people each make a promise to each other. If either of the two people breaks their oath the promise that was created between them is broken as well. If one of the two people commits adultery, they have broken their promise to the other, and that oath of marriage that binds them together is broken as a result. Divorce is a simple recognition that the marriage tie has been severed. The point isn't adultery or divorce itself, but the fact that when we make a vow of marriage we are to keep that vow. And if we go back on our promise, by adultery, by abusing the other person or being cruel to them, by abandoning them, or by doing anything else that does not honor the promise of love and loyalty that we made, the marriage oath itself is broken. In my mind, Jesus wasn't trying to single adultery out as the only reason to allow a divorce, but he was saying that people had to quit using all of those loopholes to get out of the promises they made whenever the felt like doing so. Their promises had to be promises. Their word had to be their word. They had to be different.

They had to be different than the Pharisees and Sadducees.

I think Jesus made things pretty clear and simple here. Those who follow him keep the promises they make. Like salt, they change everything they touch. Like light, they reveal the truth. They don't enforce laws to control people, but they tear down walls and fences that separate us. They don't worry about enforcing the words of laws, but they spend their time fulfilling the true meaning of those laws.

As I said, I cannot guarantee that my interpretation is absolutely what Jesus meant or that any of the things I have imagined are exactly what happened that day on the hillside. I could be mistaken. But I believe it enough to stand up here, light my little candle, and say it out loud. I know that many will disagree, and some may feel that I have gone to far. It isn't the first time, and won't be the last. That happens when you try to make complicated things simple.

It is simple to understand how to follow Jesus, but it is difficult. Following Jesus is risky. It can be dangerous and lead to persecution. It goes against many things we have been told are true. Instead of focusing on securing ourselves, we focus on making sure everyone around us is cared for. Instead of building walls, we build community. Instead of hoping for peace, we work hard to create peace wherever we are. We don't do what we do to feel proud and to feel right. We do it because we want to follow. We do it because have been called to be different.

We do what we do because we are different.

Amen.

Matthew 17:1-9

# The Mountain

Up in the northeast corner of the Sea of Galilee, a mile or so past the village of Bethsaida, there is a mountain. Or, as near what you would call a mountain in that area. If you go there today, there is a parking lot nearby, and from there you walk a steep and rocky trail for about a mile and a half to get to the top of the mountain. Even with the trail, it is a tough trek. As Jesus, Peter, James, and John walked up the mountain that day there was no parking lot and no trail. It was an ideal place to go if you wanted to just get away. More and more, Jesus was looking for opportunities to get away.

A lot has happened since that day we met with the group on that hillside near the Sea of Galilee. The pressure was on. He had spent the past few years doing more teaching, healing the sick, and generally doing things that drew people to him and made the Pharisees and Sadducees angrier and angrier. He had even made two or three trips down to Jerusalem to celebrate the Passover. But he had so many followers now that even the leaders at the temple could do no more than watch, grind their teeth, and wait for their opportunity to put an end to this pretend Messiah from Galilee.

The day he taught the crowd on the hillside there was a small group of Pharisees and Sadducees there listening as well. Now, there were more. A day didn't pass without someone trying to argue with him, or try to make his followers look like fools. Sometimes the disciples made that task pretty easy. Even after traveling alongside Jesus for three years, some of them still weren't ready. They fought with each other over which of them would get to sit next to Jesus when they all got to heaven. They argued with people who preached about Jesus but weren't officially a part of their group. A few of them ran up to Jesus one day with big smiles on their faces. "We found some Greeks preaching about you but we made them cut it out!" they said. Jesus looked at them with that look; every parent knows the look. It is the look that says, "Are you kidding me? How many times do we need to go over this? Those who are not against us are with us!" Even later, when they made their last trip together to Jerusalem, they didn't seem to get it. They fell asleep while Jesus was talking to them. And when the people came to arrest Jesus, the disciples all ran away and ended up denying they even knew who he was.

Sometimes we are pretty hard on the disciples. We shake our heads at how they behaved. I mean, they were right there with Jesus. What was their problem? If they were right there with Jesus and couldn't get things straight, what are the chances we're going to figure it out? We need to remember that most of the disciples were good Jewish boys raised in good Jewish families. What Jesus was asking them to do went against most of what they had been taught in all those years of synagogue school and did all of the things they had been carefully taught should never be done. They weren't stupid. They just had a really hard time being different. I for one can understand that.

Jesus realized how difficult it was for the disciples to do what he was asking them to do, and would sometimes take them all someplace where they could be alone and he could try and help them understand things. They were doing that more frequently now, partly to get away from the increasing opposition, and partly because Jesus knew it wasn't going to be much longer before he would not be able to teach them further. One time he took them up to Caesarea Philippi, a resort area for the Romans and a place the Jewish opposition would never bother him. And now they were making their way up the side of that mountain Northeast of Bethsaida. It was still Jewish land, but the odds were that no one was going to climb that far up to give them any problems. They would find some quiet time there to talk.

And, it seems that Jesus had something else in mind for the trip. He was going to give Peter, James, and John something that would give them the strength to do what they were going to have to do very soon. He was going to give them proof that all the things he had been saying were true. Why those three and why it was just them we aren't told. Why later he made them promise to not tell anyone what they had seen we don't know either. What was important is that from that point on Peter, James, and John knew the truth.

The mountain was steep and from the top, you could see all of the northern coast of the Sea of Galilee. They could see their old homes in Bethsaida and their new home in Capernaum. They saw the hillside where Jesus had taught all those people and the place where he had fed the others. They saw the fishermen in their boats, and in the distance, they saw the valley below Mount Arbel with all of the caves where the Zealots were crafting their swords to attack the Romans. In my mind, they pointed at places and did a lot of "Remember that time we…"It had only been three years, but a lot had happened. They talked about those things behind them because it was sometimes just too scary to talk about the things that might be coming ahead of them. When Jesus tried to talk about what was coming, and what was going to happen to him, they didn't want to hear or think about it. It wasn't that they were afraid. Well, honestly, that might at least be a part of it. They looked, pointed, and talked about what once was while Jesus stood quietly beside them.

And then it happened.

In my mind, Peter was the one who noticed it first. He just always seemed to be the one that caught things more quickly. Matthew said that while they stood there:

*"He was transfigured before them. His face shone like the sun, and his clothes became as white as the light."*

If you will pardon my imagination for a second, I can see Peter poking James with his elbow saying, "Hey, dude, look at this." That's probably what I would have done anyway. They were trying to figure out what was going on when Matthew said:

*"Just then there appeared before them Moses and Elijah, talking with Jesus."*

Keep in mind that Peter, James, and John were just small-town fishermen, and were not in any way educated scholars. But even they knew that Moses and Elijah were not only the two most important figures in Jewish history, and were the two people who would one day announce the arrival of the Messiah, but the three of them knew that Moses and Elijah had both been dead for a thousand years or so. Yet, there they were.

Wow! Can you imagine? Have you ever had one of those times you were just overwhelmed by something, maybe looked up to the sky somewhere and said, "Can't you give me some kind of proof? Just give me a sign. Even a little one!" Yeah, me too. I have no idea what I might do if someone like Moses or Elijah suddenly appeared and said, "Okay, you want proof? Now you have proof." I don't know if I would fall to the ground in terror, or just stare for a few minutes before I finally mumbled, "Thank you." Honestly, I would probably do what Peter did.

After realizing what he was seeing, Peter said, "Lord, this is awesome. I'll tell you what. Why don't we set us up some tents here and we just camp and stay a while? We can set up tents for us, and one for Moses and Elijah too. What do you think? James could run down to town and bring back some food. John could help him while I set up the tents. It's nice up here. I mean, we don't really have to go back down there, do we? Can't we just stay?"

Yes, I can't blame Peter, and I would probably do the exact same thing. It is nice on the mountaintop. It is easier. Back down below everyone questions us or wants something from us, and we keep making all those stupid mistakes down there. But up here. It is safe here. Here, we have proof that we are right. Here we don't have the doubts. Up here with Moses and Elijah, we aren't afraid of anything. Here, we are safely surrounded by others who believe what we believe. It is easy here. Can't we just stay? Do I really have to leave the mountain and go back to everything else? Can't I just stay here?

I don't think Peter was being selfish, he just felt what I think most of us feel when we have one of those top-of-the-mountain experiences. Can't we just keep it going and stay up there? Why do we have to go back down? We look for more opportunities to climb mountains and find ways to feel good and avoid spending time back down there among the things that make us uncomfortable. We look for ways to be on the mountain with those who believe what we believe and avoid those who believe differently, or who might even oppose us. No, I can't blame Peter for wanting to stay. And before anyone could respond to Peter's questions, they were all reminded of why they were on that mountain. Matthew says:

*"While he was still speaking, a bright cloud covered them, and a voice from the cloud said, "This is my son, whom I love; with him I am well pleased. Listen to him!"*

God answered Peter's questions by reminding them that they weren't up on this mountain to feel good, or to somehow get away from the hardships of being a follower of Jesus. They were here to be shown, once and for all, that Jesus was the Son of God. This mountaintop experience wasn't about giving the disciples a warm and fuzzy religious experience. It was about preparing them for what was about to come; what was going to happen when they walked back down from the mountain. They were not going to be like the Pharisees and Sadducees who took the easy path and avoided the hard times. They were going to be different than the Pharisees and Sadducees. They were going to walk back down the mountain, and they would keep walking. They were not seeking some kind of emotional, religious high. They were creating change. They were different.

Some traditions say that Jesus, Moses, and Elijah talked for a while on that mountain. We don't know what they might have talked about, and I guess it really doesn't matter all that much. What Matthew told us was that when the disciples heard the voice speaking to them they were terrified and fell to the ground. Jesus walked over and touched them. He told them to not be afraid. When they looked up, Moses and Elijah were gone. In my mind, James and John started talking a mile a minute, peppering Jesus with questions about what they had just seen. Peter stood there quietly, taking it in until he looked at Jesus and said: "I think it's time to go."

On the way back down the mountain, why did Jesus tell them not to tell anyone what they had seen and heard? Why? I don't know. While I think it makes good stuff to argue about in seminary classes, I really don't think it means all that much to us here today.

I think what is important for us to see is that this trip to the mountain was a final decision point for the three disciples. Up to this point, they had followed Jesus because they believed in him because of what he had said and did. Then they had proof. The loopholes were filled. They would either follow to the end or they would not follow. It was a clear and simple choice they would make. It was not easy by any means, but clear and simple.

In the church calendar, we are about to begin the season when we remember the final days that Jesus spent with his disciples. As a part of that we will be reminded, that when the time of decision finally arrived, the disciples blew it. But, it doesn't mean they failed. We will be reminded that, over time, each one of those three men made the choice to come back and give their lives to do what they understood they had to do. They had to follow Jesus. They had to be different than the Pharisees and Sadducees. They had to be different.

We are to be different.

Amen.